1

AI Feline Fortunes: How to Make Millions with Virtual Cats and Viral Beats

By: Matthew Petchinsky

Introduction

In recent years, the digital world has experienced a seismic shift, driven by the rapid evolution of artificial intelligence. The rise of **AI-generated content** is not just a fleeting trend—it's a revolutionary movement that's fundamentally reshaping how content is created, consumed, and monetized. From written articles and images to music and full-scale video production, AI is now at the heart of a new era of creativity and automation. This transformation is enabling individuals and businesses alike to scale their content strategies at unprecedented speed and efficiency, while also unlocking powerful new ways to engage audiences across the globe.

Among the most surprising—and oddly captivating—phenomena in this space is the explosion of **AI cats, trending AI-generated music, and synthetic personalities** that are gaining traction across platforms. These AI-generated characters and assets tap directly into internet culture, where visual appeal and emotional connection reign supreme. Take, for instance, the growing number of AI-generated cat influencers that blend realism with digital charm, or AI-powered tools that can remix trending songs in seconds, creating viral hits that travel faster than traditional production cycles ever allowed. Tools like **Hailuo AI**—which produces hyper-realistic avatars and voices—and **ChatGPT**—which can generate human-like scripts, narratives, and entire content plans—are leading this charge, providing creators with a toolkit that was once the stuff of science fiction.

Amidst all this innovation, one platform stands out as the ultimate playground for AI-driven creativity: **YouTube**. With over 2 billion logged-in monthly users and an unparalleled revenue-sharing model, YouTube offers a fertile ground for monetizing AI-generated content. The platform's algorithm rewards consistency, engagement, and originality—three things that AI excels at when used correctly. Whether it's short-form videos featuring AI pets, AI-narrated documentaries, or music mashups created in minutes, YouTube gives creators the visibility, reach, and income potential needed to turn passion into profit.

AI Feline Fortunes

AI Feline Fortunes

Petchinsky

This isn't just about posting random videos—it's about building a **scalable AI-powered content empire**. Imagine a fully automated ecosystem where AI generates video ideas, writes scripts, narrates, edits, and even uploads content based on audience analytics. With the right strategy, tools, and niche selection, it's entirely possible to go from zero to six or seven figures in revenue without a traditional production team or a physical presence. This guide is your **roadmap to building a million-dollar AI content business**, step by step—from identifying winning niches and leveraging viral trends to automating production and optimizing for monetization.

We are at the dawn of a new digital renaissance. AI is not here to replace creators—it's here to **amplify their potential**. And those who understand how to ride this wave early will be the ones leading the future of digital media.

Chapter 1: The AI Cat Craze – Why Virtual Cats Go Viral

Few things have captivated the internet quite like cats. From the early days of "I Can Has Cheezburger?" memes to the viral domination of Grumpy Cat and Nyan Cat, felines have consistently proven to be the undisputed royalty of digital content. But now, in the age of artificial intelligence, this obsession has taken a new turn—**virtual, AI-generated cats** are storming the scene, captivating millions, and redefining what it means to be a "pet influencer." What is it about cats, real or virtual, that makes them so magnetically viral? And how are creators leveraging this craze to build massive audiences?

The Psychology Behind Cat Content Obsession

At the core of this phenomenon lies human psychology. Studies have shown that watching cat videos can **boost mood, reduce stress, and trigger positive emotional responses**. Cats exhibit a blend of independence, playfulness, and unpredictability that captures attention and sparks joy. Their quirky movements, expressive eyes, and aloof-yet-adorable personalities evoke strong emotional reactions—and emotional content is what thrives on social media.

Researchers from Indiana University found that people who watched cat videos felt **more energetic and positive afterward**, and they often used the content as a way to **escape negative emotions** or procrastinate productively. This emotional impact is amplified by the **"cute aggression" phenomenon**, where viewers feel overwhelmed by cuteness and react in exaggerated ways—sharing, commenting, or watching on repeat. In the digital attention economy, this behavior is gold.

When AI enters the mix, it supercharges the effect. AI-generated cats can be **customized to perfection**—enhanced expressions, exaggerated movements, or even hybrid fantasy features like glowing eyes or robotic tails—creating a surreal mix of cuteness and novelty that is nearly irresistible to viewers.

Virtual Pets in Pop Culture and Gaming

The fascination with digital animals isn't new. The concept of virtual pets has been embedded in pop culture and gaming for decades, dating back to Tamagotchi in the 90s, followed by Neopets, and later digital companions like Nintendogs or Pokémon. These experiences tapped into the same nurturing instincts and emotional connections that real pets evoke, without the real-world responsibilities.

Fast forward to today, and we're seeing a **renaissance of virtual pet content**, fueled by AI and the metaverse. AI cats are being used in games, livestreams, VTuber channels, and augmented reality experiences. Platforms like **TikTok and YouTube Shorts** are flooded with short-form videos featuring animated feline avatars engaging in funny, cute, or outrageous behaviors—many of which are generated by tools like **Hailuo AI, Kaiber, or Genmo**.

These AI cats are more than just passive animations—they can **interact with viewers, perform scripted skits, react to trending topics**, and even "speak" in synthetic voices. The line between pet and character is blurring, turning virtual cats into full-blown digital celebrities.

Case Studies of Viral AI-Generated Cats

Let's look at a few examples that highlight just how impactful AI-generated cats have become in the content landscape:

1. MechaMochi – The Cyber Cat Influencer

MechaMochi is an AI-generated cat with a futuristic design—metallic fur, neon eyes, and glitchy animations. Created using a mix of generative AI and motion graphics, this digital feline stars in a YouTube Shorts series that blends sci-fi storytelling with comedy. Within weeks of launch, MechaMochi racked up over **5 million views**, with fans demanding merchandise and lore expansion. What made MechaMochi viral was the **fusion of niche aesthetics (cyberpunk + cats)** and the creator's strategic use of trending audio and AI-generated dialogue.

2. NekoGPT – The Talking AI Cat

Built with voice synthesis and ChatGPT for dialogue, NekoGPT is an AI avatar that answers questions, delivers memes, and reacts to current events like a sarcastic feline commentator. The channel went from zero to 100K subscribers in under four months by leveraging **AI-generated scripts, viral video formats, and emotional engagement**. Viewers not only laughed at NekoGPT's antics but also developed a strange sense of attachment—as if they were following a real personality.

3. Purrfect Synth – Music-Reacting AI Cat

Purrfect Synth is a looping animation of a chill, lo-fi cat that reacts to trending songs using subtle movements, blinking eyes, and tail flicks. The twist? It's entirely generated through AI, including the background, animation, and reaction sync. Each new video features the cat grooving to a new viral track, and the simple, soothing nature of the content drove **massive engagement** across YouTube Shorts and Instagram Reels. The formula was simple but effective: trending music + relaxing visuals + adorable AI design = repeatable virality.

Why This Trend Matters for Creators

The AI cat craze is more than a niche—it's a **blueprint for engagement**. By tapping into internet psychology, pop culture nostalgia, and cutting-edge AI tools, creators can produce content that not only entertains but builds loyal followings. AI cats are:

- **Shareable**: People love sending cute or funny cat videos to friends.
- **Scalable**: AI tools allow for mass content production with minimal effort.
- **Monetizable**: From ads and sponsorships to merch and NFTs, AI cats are a branding opportunity.
- **Evergreen**: Cat content never goes out of style.

Creators who recognize this pattern and learn to harness it using automation, creativity, and emotional intelligence can build high-performing channels with speed and efficiency.

In Summary

The AI cat craze is more than a novelty—it's a manifestation of deep psychological triggers, cultural trends, and technological innovation. As AI continues to evolve, so too will the digital creatures it brings to life. And in this emerging space, those who act early and smartly have the opportunity to **ride the viral wave straight to the top of the content economy**. Whether you're building a brand around a single digital cat or launching a whole universe of virtual pets, the potential is massive—and it's only just beginning.

Chapter 2: Choosing Your Niche – From Cute to Chaos

In the rapidly growing world of AI-generated content, especially when it comes to virtual pets like AI cats, *niche selection* is one of the most critical decisions you'll make. While cats may rule the internet, not all AI cats are created equal. The market is flooded with content—from hyper-realistic felines curled up by digital fireplaces to glitchy, demonic cyber-cats that growl in binary. Success lies in identifying a **unique angle** that not only resonates with your target audience but also aligns with your creative goals and monetization strategy.

Welcome to the world of **cat personas**, audience psychology, and digital branding—where "adorable" and "chaotic" can both be goldmines if leveraged correctly.

The Spectrum of AI Cat Personas

When creating your AI cat brand, you have the freedom to break beyond biological realism. AI lets you design cats that are not bound by physical limitations or typical behaviors. This opens up a wide creative playground of styles and niches, each attracting a different kind of audience.

Here's a breakdown of the **most compelling AI cat personas**, and how they function in today's content landscape:

1. The Adorable Companion

- **Aesthetic**: Round eyes, soft fur, warm colors, kitten-like proportions.
- **Personality**: Gentle, silly, affectionate.
- **Content Style**: Daily affirmations, wholesome reactions, cozy backgrounds, ASMR.
- **Target Audience**: Kids, families, mental wellness audiences, and cozy-core communities.
- **Why It Works**: Adorable AI cats tap into universal emotional comfort. They're ideal for generating repeat engagement and long watch time due to their soothing, binge-worthy nature.

2. The Creepy Glitch Cat

- **Aesthetic**: Asymmetrical eyes, distorted animations, horror-movie lighting.
- **Personality**: Unpredictable, surreal, eerie, often silent.
- **Content Style**: Short horror clips, analog-style glitches, "found footage" stories.
- **Target Audience**: Horror fans, ARG (Alternate Reality Game) communities, Gen Z meme culture.
- **Why It Works**: The rise of "weirdcore" and horror on platforms like TikTok and YouTube Shorts creates a space where unsettling AI cats thrive—especially when mixed with suspenseful storytelling.

3. The Mystical Oracle Cat

- **Aesthetic**: Glowing eyes, floating animations, mystical symbols, celestial themes.
- **Personality**: Wise, cryptic, otherworldly.
- **Content Style**: Tarot readings, astrological insights, cryptic riddles, ASMR oracle sessions.
- **Target Audience**: Spiritual audiences, astrology enthusiasts, fantasy lovers.
- **Why It Works**: By blending mysticism with feline charm, you create a niche that feels magical and personal. These AI cats are often seen as guides or mascots, perfect for community building.

4. The Cyberpunk Hacker Cat

- **Aesthetic**: Metallic fur, glitch overlays, neon lights, robotic movements.
- **Personality**: Sassy, tech-savvy, rebellious.
- **Content Style**: Tech rants, pop culture breakdowns, satirical hot takes, gamer content.
- **Target Audience**: Tech enthusiasts, gamers, meme lovers, anime fans.
- **Why It Works**: This type of AI cat becomes a *digital influencer*—a character who reacts to real-world tech trends or gaming culture, allowing for trending, fast-turnaround content.

5. The Chaos Cat

- **Aesthetic**: Cartoonish or absurdist design, unpredictable behavior.
- **Personality**: Loud, manic, meme-fueled.
- **Content Style**: Rapid-cut humor, absurd scenarios, meme remixes, sound overload.
- **Target Audience**: Gen Z, meme culture, short-form addicts.
- **Why It Works**: Chaos cats create *scroll-stopping* content. Their wild energy plays into TikTok humor and meme virality. Think "cat yeeting itself into space to a bass drop"—random, repeatable, and hilarious.

Understanding Audience Engagement and Retention

Once you've chosen a persona, the next step is understanding how your target audience interacts with content. Every niche has **different expectations and behavioral patterns**, and knowing these can help you tailor your AI cat to maximize watch time, shares, and subscriptions.

Here's how to break it down:

1. Emotional Triggers

- **Adorable cats** evoke calmness, nostalgia, and joy—perfect for long-form or looping content.
- **Creepy or chaotic cats** evoke surprise, fear, or laughter—ideal for short bursts of viral energy.
- Use these emotional hooks to determine your pacing, music, and editing style.

2. Viewer Behavior

- Audiences watching for comfort (adorable, mystical cats) tend to rewatch or leave videos on in the background.
- Meme/horror audiences thrive on fast scrolls and **shock-value thumbnails**.
- Engagement often spikes in comments for AI cats that "talk back" or challenge viewers (e.g., "Comment your favorite number and I'll tell you your fate").

3. Retention Metrics

- Keep your **hook strong in the first 3 seconds**.
- Use **predictable formats** (e.g., "Mystic Cat Mondays") to create habit loops.
- Add subtle Easter eggs or cliffhangers to keep viewers coming back ("Did you see the ghost in the mirror?").

How to Make Your AI Cat Stand Out from the Crowd

With the growing number of AI cat channels, originality is essential. Your cat needs to feel like a *character*, not just an animation. Here's how to make your AI cat stand out:

1. Develop Lore and Personality

- Give your AI cat a backstory: Are they from a dystopian future? A reincarnated oracle? A bug in the simulation?
- Speak in a unique voice (tone, vocabulary, or literal voice synthesis).
- Let them "grow" over time with narrative arcs, upgrades, or character development.

2. Invest in Visual Identity

- Use AI tools like **Midjourney**, **Runway**, or **Kaiber** to generate consistent design aesthetics.
- Customize accessories, backgrounds, and environments to match the cat's theme.
- Create a distinct color palette or animation style that becomes instantly recognizable.

3. Build a Brand, Not Just a Video

- Create a name, logo, intro/outro theme music.
- Use catchphrases or running jokes.
- Design your thumbnails and titles around your cat's personality—people should recognize it even in a sea of content.

4. Engage With Your Audience In-Character

- Let your cat respond to comments as if it's real.
- Ask followers for suggestions on outfits, storylines, or upgrades.
- Run polls or mini-games (e.g., "Choose which portal the mystical cat should enter next").

In Summary

Choosing the right niche for your AI cat is a creative and strategic balancing act. You're not just picking a style—you're **building a personality, an audience experience, and ultimately a brand**. Whether you lean into the heart-melting charm of an adorable kitten or the glitchy chaos of a digital monster, success lies in your ability to *commit* to a theme, understand your audience's psychology, and continuously deliver engaging, high-quality content.

Your digital empire begins with one unforgettable cat.

Chapter 3: The AI Toolkit – Essential Platforms to Use

So, you've chosen your niche. Maybe you're leaning toward a mystical, galaxy-trotting feline with glowing eyes, or perhaps you're ready to unleash a hyperactive chaos cat that roasts viewers in meme-speak. Now comes the critical next step: **bringing your AI cat to life**.

Thanks to the rapid evolution of AI tools, creating content has never been easier—or more scalable. From **text-to-animation platforms** and **voice generation tools** to **automated editing pipelines**, today's technology allows you to produce engaging, professional-quality videos at scale, often while you sleep.

This chapter breaks down the **essential AI platforms** that you can use to build a fully-automated content production system—turning one virtual cat into an unstoppable content empire.

1. Core AI Platforms to Know

Let's start with the heavy-hitters—the tools that form the foundation of your workflow.

1.1 Hailuo AI – Hyper-Realistic Avatars & Lip-Sync Video

- **What it does**: Hailuo AI specializes in generating **lifelike digital avatars** that can speak in sync with your audio. You can customize their appearance, outfit, gestures, and even emotional tone.
- **Why it's essential**: If your AI cat has a humanoid persona or speaks directly to the audience (like a VTube-style character), Hailuo is an ideal front-facing platform.
- **Pro Tip**: Use Hailuo for your cat's "storytime," reaction, or voice-over clips. You can even blend it with cat-shaped avatars to create talking AI cats.

1.2 ChatGPT – Scriptwriting & Creative Dialogue

- **What it does**: ChatGPT (especially with GPT-4) is your go-to tool for writing **video scripts, skits, captions, descriptions**, and even entire storyline arcs.
- **Why it's essential**: It saves hours of brainstorming, adapts to trends in real-time, and helps keep your cat's personality consistent across videos.
- **Pro Tip**: Use prompts like "Write a sarcastic 30-second rant in the voice of a cyberpunk AI cat about internet lag" or "Generate a mystical poem for a glowing cat oracle."

1.3 Deepbrain AI – Talking Avatar Generator

- **What it does**: Similar to Hailuo, Deepbrain AI generates **speaking avatars** from plain text input. It's highly customizable and offers fast rendering for YouTube-ready videos.
- **Why it's essential**: It's useful for talking cats, especially if you're leaning into **daily wisdom, news recaps, or commentary formats.**
- **Pro Tip**: Combine Deepbrain with a static or looped animated cat image for a fast, affordable way to bring your AI cat to life.

1.4 Runway ML – AI Video Editing & Animation

- **What it does**: Runway is a creative AI suite that includes **video editing, motion tracking, background generation, and green screen removal**—all powered by AI.
- **Why it's essential**: Perfect for editing AI-generated cat clips, adding background animations, and layering text or effects.
- **Pro Tip**: Use Runway's motion brush to animate a static cat and place it in dynamic scenes (like dancing on Mars or floating through a dreamscape).

1.5 Pika Labs / Kaiber – Text-to-Video Animation Tools

- **What they do**: These tools turn written prompts or static images into animated videos. Want your AI cat surfing a rainbow or glitching through a virtual city? These platforms make it happen.
- **Why they're essential**: They're perfect for **background loops, surreal environments, and stylized short-form content**.
- **Pro Tip**: Use them for intro scenes, transitions, or surreal moments in your video where your cat needs to "do something wild."

2. Tools for Realistic Cat Animation

Animating a believable or captivating AI cat is no longer a task limited to Pixar studios. Here's how to create your animated feline star:

2.1 Adobe Character Animator + AI Motion Capture

- **What it does**: Lets you animate characters (including cats) using your webcam or audio input.
- **Why it's useful**: Gives your cat real-time movement and lip sync using facial tracking or pre-recorded voiceovers.
- **Pro Tip**: Combine a custom cat rig with your voice and let Adobe animate it live—or use recordings for more polished control.

2.2 Animaze / VTube Studio

- **What it does**: Used by VTubers to control virtual avatars in real-time.
- **Why it's useful**: If your AI cat is a VTuber or "digital influencer," this is your control panel for streaming, YouTube content, and even TikTok Live.
- **Pro Tip**: Use a pre-built cat model or upload a custom AI-generated design for a fully interactive experience.

2.3 Genmo.ai – Generative Cat Animations

- **What it does**: Turns static images into animated short clips using AI. You upload your cat image and give it movement.
- **Why it's useful**: Great for looped animations, music syncing, or reaction gifs.
- **Pro Tip**: Combine with trending music clips for viral Shorts or Reels.

3. Automating Scriptwriting, Voiceovers & Captions

Automation is what turns your AI cat into a *scalable brand*. Here's how to build a content factory that can operate while you sleep:

3.1 Scriptwriting with ChatGPT or Claude AI

- Use pre-set prompt templates to generate daily scripts:
    - *"Give me a 30-second motivational quote from a mystical AI cat about chasing dreams."*
    - *"Write a meme-style roast of Monday mornings from a digital cat's POV."*

3.2 AI Voice Generation with ElevenLabs or PlayHT

- **What it does**: Produces ultra-realistic, customizable voiceovers.
- **Use case**: Give your AI cat a signature voice—soothing, sarcastic, robotic, or even multilingual.
- **Pro Tip**: You can clone your voice or create a completely fictional one that matches your cat's vibe.

3.3 Auto Captions & Subtitles with Captions.ai or VEED.io

- Auto-generate captions in various styles with proper pacing, emojis, and even effects.
- Great for vertical videos where captions drive retention.

3.4 Auto-Editing Pipelines with Pictory or Descript

- Upload your script + voice, and these tools will:
    - Match stock or AI visuals
    - Add transitions
    - Generate subtitles
    - Export in vertical or horizontal formats
- **Pro Tip**: Set templates for your content type (e.g., "reaction," "motivation," or "news") to maintain brand consistency.

4. The Complete Workflow – From Text to Fully Edited Video (While You Sleep)

Here's a simplified breakdown of a **repeatable content creation pipeline** that runs on automation:

1. **Idea + Script**: Use ChatGPT to generate 2–3 scripts per day based on trends.
2. **Voiceover**: Feed the script into ElevenLabs to generate your cat's voice.
3. **Animation**: Import voice into Deepbrain or Character Animator for a speaking cat.
4. **Visuals & Background**: Use Pika Labs, Runway, or Kaiber for animated settings.
5. **Editing**: Use Pictory or Runway to compile and polish the final video.
6. **Captions**: Add subtitles with Captions.ai or VEED.io.
7. **Upload**: Use TubeBuddy or vidIQ for optimized titles, descriptions, and thumbnails.
8. **Schedule**: Batch upload to YouTube and schedule for automated release.

You can set this up to produce **3–10 videos per day** with minimal manual input once your templates and personas are defined.

In Summary

With the right toolkit, creating high-quality AI cat content is no longer limited by time, talent, or technical skills. Whether you're building an adorable digital pet, a sarcastic glitch beast, or a wise feline oracle, AI platforms now allow you to **automate and scale the entire content pipeline**—from concept to final upload.

This chapter gives you the blueprint. The next step is **execution and iteration**.

Chapter 4: AI-Powered Music – Creating Trendy Tracks for Maximum Reach

In the race to go viral, **music is the heartbeat of content**. A catchy beat, a trending sound, or the perfect mood track can be the difference between a forgettable upload and a million-view hit. When it comes to AI-generated content—especially AI cat videos—music plays a massive role in **viewer retention, emotional impact, and algorithmic favor**. The good news? You don't need to be a producer or buy expensive music rights. AI is making it possible to create **viral-ready music** in minutes, tailor-made for your content, brand, and audience.

In this chapter, we'll explore how to generate trending music with AI, the top platforms you can use, and how to **integrate music strategically into your cat content**. We'll also dive into **copyright-safe practices**, and how YouTube's algorithm treats music—so you can ride the rhythm all the way to monetization.

1. Why Music Matters in AI Cat Content

AI cats, as engaging as they are visually, become exponentially more powerful when paired with the right audio. Music enhances the storytelling, sets tone, evokes emotion, and most importantly—it increases **viewer retention and shareability**.

Whether it's:

- A lo-fi beat behind an adorable kitten sleeping,
- A dramatic score for a mystical oracle cat's prophecy,
- Or a glitch-hop banger behind a chaos cat flipping through dimensions...

Music gives your content rhythm, energy, and viral potential.

The Psychology of Sound

- Music creates **emotional memory hooks**—audiences remember your cat based on how the video made them *feel*.
- High BPM (beats per minute) and sync with visuals boost retention and watch time, especially on **YouTube Shorts**.
- Catchy sound loops often lead to **rewatches** and **user interaction**—"What's that song?" comments are engagement gold.

2. Best AI Music Generators for Viral Content

Here are the most powerful and creator-friendly platforms that allow you to **generate original music with AI**—perfect for YouTube videos, Shorts, and Reels.

2.1 Soundraw

- **What it does**: Lets you create music by choosing a mood, genre, length, and instruments.
- **Best for**: Background tracks, lo-fi vibes, cinematic scores.
- **Why it rocks**: Commercial-use license included, meaning no copyright issues.

2.2 Mubert

- **What it does**: Uses AI to generate **infinite music loops** in real-time.
- **Best for**: Short-form content like TikTok/Shorts.
- **Standout feature**: Offers pre-labeled "Content Creator" licensing that's safe for YouTube.

2.3 AIVA (Artificial Intelligence Virtual Artist)

- **What it does**: Composes complex pieces with classical, cinematic, or pop influences.
- **Best for**: Story-driven videos with rich emotion (mystical cat arcs, dramatic skits).
- **Bonus**: Gives more customization than most platforms.

2.4 Beatoven.ai

- **What it does**: Cuts AI-generated music into different moods or scenes.
- **Best for**: Long-form videos with narrative shifts or multiple segments.
- **Strength**: Easy scene-based control for emotional flow.

2.5 Boomy

- **What it does**: Lets you create full songs (including vocals) with a few clicks.
- **Best for**: Creating your cat's **theme song**, intros, outros, or even meme tracks.
- **Social bonus**: Boomy songs can be uploaded to Spotify and TikTok as original music.

3. Integrating AI Music into Your Cat Videos

Music isn't just background noise—**it's a character in your story**. Here's how to strategically embed it into your workflow:

A. Match Music to Your Cat's Persona

- **Adorable/Lo-Fi Cats**: Use chillhop, ambient, or acoustic.
- **Mystical Cats**: Ethereal pads, orchestral, or dreamy electronic.
- **Chaos Cats**: Dubstep, hyperpop, glitchcore, or meme tracks.
- **Cyberpunk Cats**: Synthwave, dark techno, and digital fusion beats.

B. Sync to Visuals for Impact

- Use AI editing tools like **Runway** or **CapCut Pro** to sync visual transitions, expressions, or jumps to beat drops.
- Add sound-reactive elements like flickering eyes, glowing backgrounds, or screen glitches for chaotic cat styles.

C. Brand with Music

- Create a **recurring intro/outro theme** to make your videos instantly recognizable.
- Add background music loops for certain series (e.g., "Oracle Thursday" has its own vibe).

4. Licensing AI Music Properly to Avoid Copyright Strikes

YouTube's Content ID system is notoriously strict. Even if a song sounds AI-generated, if it's flagged, your video could be demonetized or muted.

How to Avoid Issues:

1. **Use platforms with creator licensing**:
    - **Mubert, Soundraw, Beatoven, and Boomy** all offer royalty-free commercial licenses with their subscriptions.
    - Download and store license documentation for each track in case YouTube requests proof.
2. **Avoid using "AI covers" of popular songs** unless you plan to disable monetization. Even if AI creates it, the melody might trigger Content ID.
3. **Double-check attribution requirements**. Some platforms ask you to credit the music source or link back.
4. **Create your own music** using tools like Boomy and upload to **YouTube Music or TikTok Sounds** to use it freely in your own videos.

5. YouTube: The Ultimate Music-Content Powerhouse

Pairing AI music with AI cat videos is powerful—but **YouTube** is the machine that turns them into money. Here's how to crack the algorithm and fully monetize your content:

A. Optimize for Shorts (15s–60s)

- Use trending beats or AI music that *sounds like* a trend but is royalty-free.
- Hook viewers in the **first 1.5 seconds** with music + visual synergy.
- Keep music loops tight and match visuals to the rhythm.

B. Long-Form Monetization

- Use AI music as **background scoring** to build emotional tone and professionalism.
- Add musical transitions between scenes or "chapter" moments.
- Avoid sudden volume changes—balance music and voiceover carefully for retention.

C. Build a Music Identity

- Add your cat's original music to your YouTube Audio Library for reuse.
- Create a **playlist of your AI music-powered videos**.
- Use Shorts and Community Posts to promote original songs (turning music into a second monetized asset).

6. Scaling Music Content While You Sleep

Just like the video pipeline, you can **automate your music production**:

1. **Create music with Mubert or Soundraw** using presets aligned with your cat's themes.
2. **Schedule uploads** with content using the same BPM or vibe.
3. **Auto-insert music in templates** using Descript, Runway, or CapCut.
4. **Use AI tools to generate captions** that sync with lyrics or beat drops.
5. **Batch and recycle** music clips across multiple platforms (Shorts, TikTok, Instagram Reels).

In Summary

AI music is no longer an optional add-on—it's a **core strategy for content virality**. The right track can skyrocket your AI cat video's reach, create lasting brand identity, and keep you safe from copyright issues. With tools like Soundraw, Boomy, and Mubert, you're equipped to produce infinite music loops, emotional scores, and even theme songs—all tailored to your feline star.

When paired with YouTube's Shorts discovery engine and long-form monetization, AI-generated music becomes a *scalable asset*—one that fuels both creativity and revenue.

Chapter 5: The YouTube Algorithm Hack – Making AI Cats Unstoppable

You've designed your AI cat, given it a unique personality, scored it with catchy AI-generated music, and created a visually stunning video. But how do you make sure it *gets seen*? The answer lies in understanding and mastering **YouTube's algorithm**—a dynamic, data-driven system designed to serve content people want to watch, engage with, and share.

This chapter will give you the **algorithm blueprint**, show you how to craft irresistible thumbnails and titles, teach you how to maximize watch time and viewer retention, and walk you through the **monetization pathways** that turn AI-generated cat videos into serious income streams.

Let's make your AI cat not just go viral—but become **algorithmically unstoppable**.

1. The Secret to Getting Recommended by YouTube's Algorithm

YouTube's algorithm has one primary goal: **keep viewers on the platform**. That means your content must do two things exceptionally well:

1. **Attract clicks (CTR – Click-Through Rate)**
2. **Keep people watching (AVD – Average View Duration & Retention)**

The algorithm is less concerned with *what* your video is about, and more focused on **how people react to it**.

Key Ranking Factors:

- **CTR (Click-Through Rate)**: If people don't click, YouTube won't push your video.
- **Retention**: If viewers drop off before 30 seconds, YouTube sees that as a red flag.
- **Engagement**: Comments, likes, shares, and rewatches = algorithmic love.
- **Consistency**: The more consistently you post, the more likely you'll get into the algorithm's "trusted creator" loop.

For AI Cat Channels Specifically:

- Quirky visuals, mystery, and short-format "shock + delight" moments are ideal.
- Cats are inherently engaging—use this to your advantage with personality-driven content that evokes emotion, surprise, or humor.

2. Clickbait vs. Curiosity: Winning the Thumbnail and Title Game

A. Clickbait is Dead. Curiosity Wins.

Clickbait may get you a short-term spike, but **YouTube punishes bounce rates**. The real hack? Create thumbnails and titles that spark **curiosity without deception**.

B. The Thumbnail Formula

Thumbnails should:

- **Be emotionally expressive** (big eyes, dramatic reactions, vivid backgrounds)
- **Create a visual question** (e.g., "What is this cat doing in a space suit?")
- **Avoid clutter** (1–2 focal points max)
- **Be branded** (use consistent font, colors, and your AI cat's visual signature)

◈ *Example:*

Mystical Cat Oracle video
Title: "This AI Cat Predicted Your Future (It's Weirdly Accurate...)"
Thumbnail: Glowing cat with third eye, tarot cards flying, shocked emoji-style expression.

C. Title Strategies That Work

- **Mystery Hooks**: "What This Cat Did at 3AM Shocked Me"
- **Story Promises**: "A Day in the Life of a Glitched Cat from the Future"
- **Challenge Formats**: "I Let an AI Cat Run My Life for 24 Hours"
- **Emotional Pulls**: "This Cat Is Too Pure for This World..."

3. Strategies to Keep Viewers Engaged Beyond 30 Seconds

Viewer retention is your *golden metric*. The more time viewers spend with your AI cat, the more YouTube promotes your content.

A. Strong Hooks (0–10 Seconds)

- Open with action, emotion, or humor.
- Use movement, sound cues, or your cat "talking" directly to the viewer.
- Tease the outcome: "Wait until you see what happens at the end!"

B. Pacing and Pattern Interrupts

- Change visuals or zoom every 5–7 seconds.
- Use music shifts, sound effects, and cuts to keep momentum.
- Add on-screen text or reactions from your cat to emphasize moments.

C. Interactive Elements

- Ask questions early on: "Would you trust this AI cat with your secrets?"
- Use polls, comments, or viewer challenges: "Comment 'MEOW' if you made it this far!"

D. Episodic Content

- Create **series or story arcs** that hook viewers into the next video.
- Use cliffhangers or preview the next episode in the last 5 seconds.

4. YouTube Monetization Blueprint: Turn Views into Revenue

Once your content is engaging and discoverable, it's time to **monetize like a pro**. YouTube offers multiple income streams for AI creators—and with the right setup, your AI cat could be your digital cash machine.

A. AdSense Revenue (YouTube Partner Program)

- **Eligibility**: 1,000 subscribers + 4,000 watch hours or 10M Shorts views in 90 days.
- Once approved, you earn from:
  - Pre-roll, mid-roll, and post-roll ads
  - Shorts ad revenue (split from Shorts fund)

◈ *Tip*: Shorter videos = higher CPM with trending topics. Longer videos (8+ min) = multiple ad breaks = more $$.

B. Super Chats & Channel Memberships

- Enable once you're monetized.
- Live streams with your AI cat using VTube avatars or animation loops can drive **super chats and donations**.
- Offer exclusive content, emoji, or "early access" for members.

C. Merch Integration

- Add branded merch below your videos once you hit eligibility.
- Ideas: Cat plushies, themed stickers, voiceover soundboards, or "AI cat tarot" decks.
- Use services like **Spring**, **Printful**, or **Shopify** with YouTube integration.

D. Sponsorships & Brand Deals

- Once you gain traction, niche brands (pet products, AI tools, gaming gear) may approach you—or you can pitch them.
- Use a media kit and highlight your cat's engagement, reach, and audience loyalty.
- Bonus: AI cats are **non-controversial mascots**—a major plus for brands looking to avoid drama-prone influencers.

E. Affiliate Marketing

- Promote gear you use to make your videos (microphones, editing tools, cat avatars).
- Use affiliate links in video descriptions and comment pins.
- Example: "This is the voice generator I used for FluffBot's speech—try it here!"

5. Bonus: Algorithm-Friendly Publishing Habits

To stay in the good graces of the YouTube algorithm:

- **Post consistently** (at least 2–3 times per week to start)
- **Respond to comments early** (engagement boosts ranking)
- **Use YouTube Analytics** to monitor CTR, retention, and top traffic sources
- **Double-down on what works**—repurpose high-performing Shorts into long-form, or vice versa
- **Create playlists** to increase watch sessions (e.g., "Mystic Mondays," "FluffBot Rants," etc.)

In Summary

Cracking the YouTube algorithm isn't about cheating the system—it's about **understanding what the system rewards**: engagement, consistency, originality, and emotional connection. With AI-generated cats, you already have a powerful, flexible character to build around. Add strong music, smart editing, clickable thumbnails, and a monetization strategy, and you're not just playing the game—you're winning it.

When done right, your AI cat can evolve from a digital experiment into a full-blown **media brand**—earning revenue while entertaining the world 24/7.

Chapter 6: Monetization Mastery – Turning AI Cat Videos into Millions

Creating AI-generated cat videos isn't just an exercise in creativity—it's a business opportunity with the potential to generate **massive, diversified income streams**. With the right systems in place, you can turn your virtual feline into a digital cash machine, earning from YouTube AdSense, sponsorships, NFTs, affiliate links, and even **memberships and metaverse integrations**.

This chapter will walk you through a complete monetization blueprint, showing you how to **optimize YouTube revenue**, diversify across platforms, and **build a scalable brand that prints money while you sleep**.

1. YouTube AdSense – Maximizing Your Revenue Per View

Once you've joined the **YouTube Partner Program**, you gain access to AdSense, which pays you for the ads shown before, during, or after your videos.

Key Metrics That Impact Your Revenue

- **CPM (Cost Per Mille)**: How much advertisers pay per 1,000 views. Varies by niche, region, and audience demographics.
- **RPM (Revenue Per Mille)**: How much *you* actually earn per 1,000 views after YouTube's cut.
- **Watch Time**: Longer watch time = more ad slots = more revenue.

How to Optimize Ad Revenue:

- **Create longer-form videos (8+ minutes)** to enable multiple ad breaks.
- **Use storytelling** and multi-part episodes to increase average view duration (AVD).
- **Target high-CPM niches** (tech, finance, AI, education) by incorporating relevant themes into your cat's world. Example: "FluffBot breaks down the Bitcoin crash."
- **Appeal to global audiences** but cater to monetized countries like the US, UK, Canada, and Australia.
- **Use Shorts for rapid growth**, but lean on long-form for higher earnings.

◈ **Pro Tip**: Use AI tools like ChatGPT to generate scripts optimized for high-retention storytelling formats.

2. Alternative Revenue Streams: Beyond AdSense

To truly master monetization, you need to diversify. Here are the **six most profitable revenue streams** for AI cat creators:

A. Sponsorships and Brand Deals

- Partner with brands that align with your cat's niche or tone (pet products, tech gear, AI software, gamer accessories).
- Build a **creator media kit** highlighting your audience demographics, views, and engagement.
- Pitch brands directly via platforms like **Collabstr, CreatorIQ, or BrandSnob**.
- Negotiate flat fees, revenue splits, or product bundles.

◈ Example: "This episode of Oracle Cat is brought to you by [AI Tarot App]—your digital destiny awaits."

B. Affiliate Marketing

- Promote tools you use to make your videos (AI voice generators, animation tools, editing software).
- Use shortened, trackable links in your descriptions and pinned comments.
- Focus on **recurring commissions** (e.g., subscriptions to tools like ElevenLabs, Runway, etc.)

◈ Example: "Want your own AI cat voice? I used this voice generator [affiliate link]!"

C. Digital Products

- Sell assets related to your cat's brand:
    - Wallpapers, stickers, digital trading cards
    - AI-generated soundboards or cat voice packs
    - "Behind-the-scenes" creator templates
- Use platforms like **Gumroad, Ko-fi, or Payhip** to host and deliver digital goods.

D. Merch Store

- Launch branded merch through **Printful, Teespring, or Shopify**:
    - Plushies, mugs, shirts with your AI cat's face or quotes
    - Limited-edition "glitched" merch drops for chaos cat fans
- Integrate directly with YouTube's merch shelf for visibility under your videos.

E. Memberships and Subscriptions

- Activate **YouTube Memberships** and offer exclusive content:
    - Bonus videos
    - "Ask the Cat" Q&A streams
    - Member-only chat during live premieres
- Expand to **Patreon** or **Ko-fi Gold** for deeper tiered access.

◈ Incentivize with digital rewards: exclusive wallpapers, secret lore, or sneak peeks at upcoming videos.

F. Super Chats and Live Tips

- Host **livestreams** with your AI cat (using tools like VTube Studio or OBS).
- Let your cat "react" to comments, play games, or do fortune-telling live.
- Enable Super Chat and live tipping to drive direct revenue from engagement.

3. Creating AI Cat NFTs & Web3 Integration

As blockchain tech continues to evolve, digital creators are monetizing in new ways—enter **NFTs and collectibles**.

How to Get Started with AI Cat NFTs:

- Design limited-edition NFTs using platforms like **OpenSea, Rarible, or Zora**.
- Offer:
  - Unique art pieces of your cat
  - Collectible animations
  - Unlockable content or access to private content streams
- Tie NFTs to **real-world utility** (e.g., holders get voting rights on future story arcs, exclusive merch, or access to a members-only Discord).

⟐ Be transparent about value and avoid overpromising. Build *community* first, then offer digital collectibles with meaningful connection to your content.

4. Building a Cross-Platform AI Cat Empire

Don't stop at YouTube. To scale your brand into a **multi-platform juggernaut**, here's how to expand smartly:

A. TikTok

- Repurpose Shorts or behind-the-scenes clips.
- Use trending audio and hashtags (#AIcat, #FYP, #DigitalPet).
- Engage with duets, stitches, and fast reaction trends to grow fast.

◈ TikTok virality = massive subscriber funnel for YouTube.

B. Instagram Reels & Stories

- Use Reels to share polished, branded clips.
- Share personal "cat lore" or funny moments in Stories to build parasocial bonds.
- Add product links via the shop tab for digital or physical merch.

C. Streaming on Twitch or Kick

- Turn your AI cat into a **virtual streamer** using VTuber software.
- Stream live AMA sessions, "AI cat reacts" to current events, or chill lo-fi streams with animated loops.
- Monetize with tips, subs, and sponsors.

D. Discord Community

- Build a private community around your cat brand:
    - Share exclusive content
    - Hold fan events (e.g., "Design your own AI cat contest")
    - Create channels for lore, memes, fan art, and music.

◈ Use this to **nurture superfans** who will support you on Patreon, buy NFTs, and evangelize your content.

E. The Metaverse & Virtual Worlds

- Deploy your AI cat avatar in virtual spaces like **VRChat, Decentraland, or Spatial**.
- Host interactive meetups, storytelling events, or NFT drops.
- Offer AR filters or 3D assets for fans to use in their own content.

5. Building a Monetization Flywheel

Here's how all your income streams feed into each other:

1. **YouTube Ad Revenue** gives you base income and audience growth.
2. **Cross-platform promotion** brings in new followers and boosts algorithm performance.
3. **Sponsorships and affiliate links** monetize even views that don't generate AdSense.
4. **Merch and digital products** let fans financially support your cat's world.
5. **NFTs and memberships** create exclusivity and community loyalty.
6. **Streaming and Discord** add interactivity and live monetization potential.

◈ When done right, this ecosystem becomes a **self-sustaining empire** that grows with every video, every share, and every superfan.

In Summary

Monetizing your AI cat isn't just about making a few bucks from ads—it's about **building an ecosystem** where every view, every click, and every fan interaction can turn into value. From traditional revenue like AdSense and sponsorships to cutting-edge digital collectibles and cross-platform growth, there's never been a better time to launch a **high-impact AI brand**.

With strategic tools, creative flair, and a bit of hustle, your AI cat can go from a virtual pet to a **seven-figure powerhouse**—leading a brand that exists across YouTube, TikTok, NFTs, merch lines, and even the metaverse.

Chapter 7: Shorts vs. Long-Form Videos – The Ultimate Content Strategy

In the realm of AI-generated cat content, creating videos is only part of the game. The real magic lies in **how you deploy them**. The most successful content empires on YouTube—and across social media—understand that different formats serve different purposes. **YouTube Shorts** and **long-form videos** each offer unique advantages, and when used together strategically, they create a powerful feedback loop of growth, engagement, and monetization.

This chapter will break down the core differences between Shorts and long-form, show you how to maximize reach with **short-form virality**, and funnel that attention into deeper engagement and revenue through long-form storytelling. We'll also look at how **daily uploads and strategic timing** amplify your algorithmic visibility, and how to **build a content production team (or AI assistant army)** so you can scale this operation without burning out.

1. The Battle Between YouTube Shorts and Traditional Videos

YouTube Shorts (videos under 60 seconds, vertical format) and traditional long-form videos (typically 3–10+ minutes, horizontal) serve different goals within your strategy.

YouTube Shorts: The Growth Engine

- **Purpose**: **Discovery.** Get in front of new viewers quickly.
- **Reach**: Can be seen by millions overnight thanks to the Shorts shelf algorithm.
- **Engagement**: Short, punchy, scroll-stopping content thrives here.
- **Monetization**: Lower RPM than long-form, but higher viral potential.
- **Best for**:
    - Quick jokes, reactions, or "cat moments"
    - Trends and challenges
    - Teasers for upcoming videos
    - Repurposing longer content

Long-Form Videos: The Monetization Hub

- **Purpose**: **Retention & Revenue.** Build loyal fans and deepen engagement.
- **Reach**: Grows more slowly but builds stronger relationships.
- **Engagement**: Higher watch time = better monetization + community building.
- **Monetization**: Ads, memberships, merch, affiliate links, and sponsorships all thrive here.
- **Best for**:
    - Story-driven content or skits
    - Tutorials or lore drops
    - Reactions, reviews, AI cat commentary
    - "A day in the life" of your AI cat

◈ Key Takeaway:

Shorts bring them in. Long-form keeps them loyal. Use Shorts to hook curiosity and long-form to build depth, personality, and revenue.

2. How to Maximize Reach with Shorts & Funnel Traffic to Long-Form

Shorts can reach millions—but you don't want to be "just another funny cat video." You want to **convert scrolls into subscribers.**

Short-Form Strategy Tips:

- **Post 1–3 Shorts daily** to increase your chance of hitting the Shorts shelf.
- **Hook fast**: Grab attention in the first 1–2 seconds with movement, music, or a question.
- **Use a cliffhanger or teaser** that leads into your long-form video.
    - *"Wait 'til you see what happened next... full video on the channel!"*
- **Add pinned comments** linking to full-length videos.
- **Use consistent characters, catchphrases, or lore** that encourage binge-watching.

Bridge Shorts to Long-Form:

- Use **Shorts as trailers** for episodic content (e.g., "FluffBot's time-travel adventure begins...")
- Post "highlight reels" from long-form videos.
- Create narrative arcs across Shorts that culminate in a long-form drop.

◈ **Pro Tip**: Add an end screen or pinned comment that says:
"Want the full story? Click here → [Link to long video]"

3. The Importance of Daily Uploads & Strategic Posting Times

Why Daily Uploads Matter

- YouTube's algorithm **rewards consistency**.
- Frequent uploads increase your chances of catching viral momentum.
- It signals to YouTube (and your audience) that your channel is active, engaged, and worth recommending.

Posting Schedule Best Practices:

- **Daily Shorts**: 1–3 per day, ideally spaced out by a few hours.
- **Long-form**: 2–4 times per week is ideal, depending on your editing workflow.
- **Go Live** once per week (even pre-recorded as a "premiere") to boost engagement and Super Chat revenue.

Best Times to Post:

- Analyze **YouTube Studio** > **Audience** tab to see when your viewers are most active.
- General timing tips:
    - **Weekdays**: Between 12PM–3PM (U.S. time zones)
    - **Weekends**: Between 9AM–11AM
    - **Shorts**: Test early morning + evening posts for highest scroll time

⟐ Use tools like **TubeBuddy** or **vidIQ** to fine-tune your upload schedule and optimize your tags and descriptions for SEO.

4. Building a Content Production Team (or AI Assistant Army)

Scaling content daily sounds overwhelming—unless you **automate it smartly** or **delegate the right pieces.**

The AI Assistant Stack – Automate First

- **Scriptwriting**: ChatGPT or Claude AI
- **Voiceovers**: ElevenLabs or PlayHT
- **Animation**: Kaiber, Genmo, Runway
- **Editing**: Pictory, CapCut Pro, Descript
- **Music**: Soundraw, Mubert
- **Captions/Subtitles**: VEED.io, Captions.ai
- **Scheduling/Upload**: YouTube Studio + Metricool or Buffer

◈ Create **templates** for video types (e.g., intro, outro, visual styles) to reduce decision fatigue and speed up production.

Hiring & Outsourcing: The Human Side
As your brand grows, consider assembling a lean team:

Role	Tasks	Where to Find
Video Editor	Final polish, adding effects, pacing	Upwork, Fiverr, Video Husky
Thumbnail Designer	Creates eye-catching visuals	99designs, Freelancer
VA (Virtual Assistant)	Uploading, tagging, managing comments	OnlineJobs.ph, Upwork
Community Manager	Discord, fan engagement, polls	Part-time social media managers

⟐ Tip: **Train with SOPs (Standard Operating Procedures)** so new team members can jump in without slowing you down.

5. Build a Content Factory Workflow

Here's how a streamlined AI-powered system could work:

1. **Brainstorm**: Use ChatGPT to generate 10 video ideas in one sitting.
2. **Script**: Use templates to generate voiceovers with ChatGPT and ElevenLabs.
3. **Visual Creation**: Use Pika Labs, Runway, or stock animation + Adobe tools.
4. **Edit**: Use CapCut or Descript with preset templates.
5. **Shorts & Long-form Split**: Turn every long-form into 2–3 Shorts using highlights.
6. **Schedule**: Upload via YouTube Studio; batch schedule for the week.
7. **Engage**: Spend 15–30 min responding to comments to boost visibility.

In Summary

The battle between Shorts and long-form isn't either/or—it's both. YouTube Shorts are your **discovery engine**, grabbing millions of eyeballs fast. Long-form content is your **monetization vehicle**, where deeper stories, higher ad rates, and community loyalty thrive. Combine them into a strategic system, powered by AI and automation, and you can grow faster, reach farther, and monetize smarter.

By **uploading daily, posting at the right times, and scaling with AI assistants or a micro-team**, you create a **repeatable machine**—one that turns your AI cat from a novelty into a fully monetized brand.

Chapter 8: AI Automation – Running a 24/7 YouTube Empire

Imagine waking up to thousands of new views, comments, and sales—all while you were asleep. This isn't a fantasy. With the power of **AI automation**, you can build and operate a fully functioning YouTube content empire that runs 24/7, producing, publishing, and optimizing content with minimal manual effort.

By strategically combining AI tools, outsourcing the right tasks, and using intelligent analytics, you can **scale your AI cat brand** into a round-the-clock operation. Even better—you'll have the time and systems to nurture a thriving fan community, turning passive viewers into **loyal superfans and brand ambassadors**.

Let's dive into how to build and run this automated empire.

1. Scaling Production with AI-Generated Content

Your AI cat doesn't sleep, doesn't get tired, and doesn't need a break. It's the perfect content engine—**as long as you feed it the right AI systems**. Here's how to scale video creation with automation:

A. The Fully Automated Video Workflow

Step	Tool	Output
Idea Generation	ChatGPT / Claude	Viral video concepts, script outlines
Scriptwriting	ChatGPT	Full video scripts in your cat's voice
Voice Generation	ElevenLabs / PlayHT	Ultra-realistic, character-specific voiceovers
Visual Animation	Kaiber, Genmo, Runway, Pika Labs	Stylized scenes, animated cat movements
Editing	Descript, CapCut Pro, Pictory	Polished video with cuts, effects, captions
Music	Soundraw, Mubert	Royalty-free, AI-generated soundtrack
Captions/Subtitles	VEED.io, Captions.ai	Auto-synced, stylized subtitles for Shorts
Scheduling	Metricool, YouTube Studio	Batch uploads and timed releases

With these tools in sync, you can **generate, edit, and publish 3–10 videos per day** without burning out. Just feed the machine—and let it purr.

B. Batch Processing: Work Smarter, Not Harder

- **Batch script** 10–20 videos in one sitting using prompts and templates.
- Generate multiple voiceovers at once with tools like **ElevenLabs Voice Cloning**.
- Use modular editing templates to plug-and-play visuals, transitions, and audio.

◈ *Pro Tip*: Create content pillars—like "Mystic Mondays," "Fluffbot Fridays," or "Chaos Cat Challenges"—to structure your calendar and streamline production.

2. Outsourcing Editing & Branding for Maximum Efficiency
Even with AI, there are times when **human touch adds polish**—especially for editing finesse, branding consistency, and audience engagement. The key is to outsource **high-skill, low-time-value tasks**, so you can focus on strategy and creativity.

A. What to Outsource

- **Video Editing**: Final polish, transitions, VFX, pacing for long-form.
- **Thumbnail Design**: Eye-catching visuals, emotional hooks, consistent branding.
- **Content Uploading**: Tagging, SEO, metadata optimization, community posts.
- **Community Management**: Comment moderation, Discord engagement, fan replies.
- **Merch & Web Design**: Product page design, shop maintenance.

B. Where to Hire

- **Upwork** – High-quality freelancers for editing, branding, VA tasks.
- **Fiverr** – Quick jobs like thumbnails, intro animations, or music loops.
- **OnlineJobs.ph** – Virtual assistants with long-term availability.
- **Internships/Student Creators** – Partner with media students for fresh, budget-friendly talent.

◈ *Build SOPs (Standard Operating Procedures)* with Loom tutorials and Google Docs so anyone can step in and execute.

3. Using AI Analytics Tools to Optimize Future Videos

Creating content is only half the battle. To grow an empire, you must **track, test, and tweak**—and AI tools can help you see patterns human eyes might miss.

Top AI-Powered Analytics Tools

Tool	Function
vidIQ	Keyword research, trending topics, competitor analysis
TubeBuddy	Tag optimization, title A/B testing, upload checklists
Metricool	Cross-platform analytics, scheduling, audience heatmaps
Peech	AI content insights: emotional tone, narrative pacing
ChatGPT (custom-trained)	Generate strategy reports from YouTube Studio data

What to Track and Optimize

- **Click-Through Rate (CTR)**: Test thumbnails and titles using A/B tools.
- **Watch Time & AVD**: Improve pacing and hooks.
- **Engagement Rate**: Use questions and CTAs to prompt more interaction.
- **Audience Demographics**: Tailor voice and topics based on viewer locations and age.
- **Traffic Sources**: Know whether Shorts, search, or recommendations are driving growth.

◈ *Turn data into strategy*: If viewers love "creepy chaos cat rants," double down with a weekly mini-series.

4. Community Building – Turning Viewers into Superfans

Content grows your channel. **Community grows your brand.**

Here's how to turn casual viewers into loyal superfans who will buy your merch, fund your Patreon, and promote your AI cat like it's their spirit animal:

A. Build a Fan Ecosystem

- **Discord Server**: The hub for real-time engagement. Create channels for memes, fan art, lore theories, and livestream chat.
- **YouTube Community Tab**: Use polls, teaser images, and sneak peeks to spark conversation.
- **Livestreaming**: Do "Ask the Cat" sessions, prophecy readings, or gaming streams in-character using VTuber tools.
- **Email List or Newsletter**: Send "Cat Chronicles" with updates, behind-the-scenes, or early access content.

B. Reward Superfans

- Launch a **fan badge or rank system** ("Chaos Cult Leader," "Mystic Knight," etc.)
- Offer **exclusive content** through Patreon or YouTube Memberships:
    - Early access
    - Secret lore videos
    - Custom voice messages from the cat
- Hold contests: "Design a new outfit for the Oracle Cat!"

C. Turn Superfans into Ambassadors

- Create a **digital street team** that:
  - Shares your videos across platforms
  - Tags your brand in memes, reels, and threads
  - Gets rewards like shout-outs, merch, or NFT drops

◈ Give them tools: branded image packs, AI-generated memes, sticker templates, even your cat's AI voice for user-generated content.

5. Your 24/7 AI Cat Empire in Motion

With all systems in place, here's what a fully automated, community-driven empire looks like:

- **AI Tools** generate content day and night
- **Virtual assistants and editors** polish, upload, and engage
- **Analytics AI** tracks performance and refines the strategy
- **Fans fuel your growth**, creating memes, lore, and conversations
- **Your AI cat becomes a brand**, not just a character

You're no longer just a content creator—you're the **CEO of a digital brand**, commanding an empire of pixels, purring processors, and superfans who spread your message across the web.

In Summary

AI automation isn't about replacing creativity—it's about **amplifying it at scale**. With the right tools and workflows, your content machine can operate 24/7, producing viral videos, growing a loyal audience, and generating passive income while you focus on vision and innovation.

By outsourcing strategically, analyzing intelligently, and building a community that *feels ownership*, you transform a virtual cat into a cultural icon. This is the future of creator entrepreneurship—and you're leading the charge.

Chapter 9: The Psychology of Engagement – Making Viewers Addicted

Virality alone doesn't build empires—**engagement does**. It's one thing to get someone to click on a cute AI cat video, but it's another to make them **watch five in a row, leave a comment, subscribe, and return tomorrow for more**. That's the power of emotional connection, psychology-backed storytelling, and intentional audience interaction.

In this chapter, we'll explore how to psychologically *hook* your viewers using AI cat personas, narrative design, and social triggers. We'll break down how to make your cat **talk, react, and bond** with your audience like a real digital friend. We'll also cover how to tap into **nostalgia and meme culture** to increase shareability, and finally, how to **future-proof your brand** as the digital ecosystem expands into AR, VR, and AI companions.

Let's dive in.

1. How to Make AI Cats "Talk" and Interact with the Audience

Your AI cat may be a digital construct, but it should feel *alive*. Viewers should feel like they're watching a **personality, not just pixels**. This is key to triggering parasocial relationships—one-sided bonds that keep viewers coming back.

A. Creating a Talking AI Cat

- **Voice Generation**:
  - Tools: **ElevenLabs**, **PlayHT**, or **Coqui Studio**
  - Create a **unique voiceprint** for your cat—soothing, sarcastic, glitchy, regal, etc.
  - Add expressive intonation: pacing, pitch, pauses for comedic or emotional effect.
- **Facial Expressions & Lip Sync**:
  - Tools: **Adobe Character Animator**, **Animaze**, **Hailuo AI**, **Deepbrain AI**
  - Sync voiceover with animated facial movements to make your cat feel present.
  - Add blinking, head tilts, tail twitches, and ear movement to mimic body language.
- **Direct Audience Interaction**:
  - Speak in the second person: "You know what I think, human?"
  - Ask questions: "Would *you* trust a glitchy cat with your secrets?"
  - Break the fourth wall occasionally to surprise and delight viewers.

◈ *Pro Tip*: Use ChatGPT to generate dynamic, in-character responses to trending topics or comments. Let your cat have *opinions*.

2. Implementing Narrative-Driven Content to Keep People Hooked

People are addicted to **stories**, not just videos. When your AI cat has a backstory, a goal, or a recurring dilemma, you create **emotional stakes** that drive binge-watching and fandom.

A. Build a Story Universe

- Give your cat an origin story:
    - Are they from the future? A failed lab experiment? A guardian of interdimensional memes?
- Introduce **side characters** or rivals: a grumpy owl oracle, a mouse hacker, a glitch-dog.
- Create **recurring segments**:
    - "Oracle Cat Thursdays" (mystical predictions)
    - "Chaos Cat Chronicles" (unhinged adventures)
    - "Tech Talk with FluffBot" (sassy takes on tech trends)

B. Use Proven Narrative Structures

- **Hero's Journey**: Your cat seeks to discover their true purpose in the digital realm.
- **Episodic Series**: Build arcs across multiple videos—each one ending with a teaser.
- **Mini-Plots in Shorts**:
    - Hook → Conflict → Resolution in under 60 seconds.
    - Example: "Cat tries to break the simulation... again."

C. Trigger Curiosity Loops

- End on cliffhangers: “What the glitch just happened? Tune in tomorrow.”
- Tease upcoming content: “I found something in the data vault... uploading soon.”
- Reward repeat viewers with hidden lore or inside jokes.

3. Leveraging Nostalgia and Memes to Boost Virality

Emotion and relatability are the two most powerful drivers of shareable content. **Nostalgia and meme culture** blend both perfectly—especially with Gen Z and Millennials, who dominate YouTube and TikTok viewership.

A. Nostalgia as a Hook

- Reference retro games, 90s/2000s cartoons, old internet culture.
- Create "AI versions" of iconic moments:
  - "What if this cat replaced Clippy from Microsoft Office?"
  - "FluffBot reacts to vintage Tamagotchi trauma."
- Use nostalgic filters, sound effects, and text overlays to trigger memory-based engagement.

B. Meme Integration

- React to or recreate trending memes—**but with a twist**:
  - Your cat reacting to "this is fine" scenarios.
  - A mystical cat doing the "Sigma stare."
  - Use "NPC behavior" jokes for robotic cat moments.
- Tools: ChatGPT for meme script ideas, CapCut for trending formats, Pictory for meme templates.

◈ *Pro Tip*: Add **meme reaction segments** into longer videos—AI cat reacts to the internet = endless content fuel.

4. Community Building: Superfans & Ambassadors

Engagement doesn't stop with the video—it continues in the comments, on Discord, and across platforms. Your goal: **turn casual viewers into ride-or-die superfans** who create content, promote your brand, and fuel long-term success.

A. Fan-Driven Engagement Strategies

- Ask fans to:
  - Name characters.
  - Submit AI art or fanfic.
  - Vote on story outcomes.
- Feature top comments or fan creations in your next video.

B. Superfan Platforms

- **Discord Server**: Offer "secret channels" for lore theories, Easter egg hunts, or early content.
- **YouTube Memberships**: Offer tiered access to:
  - Private livestreams
  - Behind-the-scenes content
  - Limited-edition digital downloads
- **NFTs and Badges**: Offer exclusive ownership and digital perks tied to fan engagement.

C. Empower Ambassadors

- Give trusted fans early access or mod roles.
- Send branded packs with voice clips, avatars, or stickers.
- Build a "Cat Crew" or "Digital Cult" that promotes you across Reddit, Twitter/X, TikTok.

5. Future-Proofing Your AI Cat Brand

To dominate long-term, your brand must **adapt and evolve** with technology and culture. Here's how to stay ahead of the curve:

A. Stay Trend-Aware

- Follow creator economy newsletters, TikTok trends, and YouTube Creator Insider updates.
- Use **AI trend prediction tools** like Glimpse or Exploding Topics.
- Test experimental formats—interactive polls, YouTube Stories, 3D Shorts.

B. Expand Into New Realms

- **AR (Augmented Reality)**:
  - Create Instagram and TikTok AR filters of your cat.
  - Partner with Lens Studio or Spark AR developers.
- **VR/Metaverse**:
  - Launch your AI cat in **VRChat, Spatial, or Decentraland.**
  - Host virtual fan meetups or digital concerts.
- **AI Companion Apps**:
  - Create a chatbot version of your cat using ChatGPT API or Replika-style platforms.
  - Fans can text or "talk" to your cat, unlocking lore or voice notes.
- **Mobile Game/Experience**:
  - Simple game mechanics: "FluffBot's Escape from the Simulation"
  - Monetize via in-app purchases or ads.

◈ *Pro Tip*: Partner with indie developers or use no-code platforms like Adalo or Bubble to test ideas fast.

In Summary

Mastering viewer engagement isn't just about creating good content—it's about **understanding human psychology**. When your AI cat speaks directly to the audience, delivers a compelling story, references memes they love, and invites them into an interactive universe, you're no longer making videos. You're building **a digital world they want to live in**.

Combine storytelling, nostalgia, interaction, and future-focused innovation, and your AI cat won't just go viral—it will become a digital icon with a **community of superfans, sustainable revenue streams, and a presence across every platform and medium**.

Chapter 10: The Social Media Expansion Strategy

Your AI cat may have started its journey on YouTube, but to build a truly unstoppable empire, you need to **expand beyond a single platform**. In today's attention economy, content needs to meet audiences *where they are*—which means spreading your brand across TikTok, Instagram Reels, Facebook Shorts, and beyond.

The goal? **Multiply visibility without multiplying your workload**. By smartly repurposing your content, cross-promoting like a pro, and using AI to handle audience interaction, you can dominate all the major platforms while focusing on scaling your core brand.

This chapter will cover your **omni-platform strategy**, complete with automation tools, engagement techniques, and a **30-day launch roadmap** to take your AI cat brand from zero to empire.

1. Repurposing AI Cat Content Across Platforms

Creating content for every platform from scratch is a recipe for burnout. The solution is **repurposing**—taking one core piece of content and adapting it for multiple channels.

A. Core Content Creation Flow

1. **Create one long-form YouTube video**
2. **Clip 2–5 viral moments** into Shorts (60s or less)
3. **Repurpose Shorts for TikTok, Instagram Reels, and Facebook Shorts**
4. **Use snippets for Stories, Community posts, or tweets**

B. Format Requirements by Platform

Platform	Max Length	Aspect Ratio	Best Practices
TikTok	3 min (ideal: <60s)	9:16 (vertical)	Trends, memes, music sync
Instagram Reels	90 sec (ideal: <30s)	9:16	High visual appeal, branded style
Facebook Shorts	60 sec	9:16	Loops well, meme-friendly
YouTube Shorts	60 sec	9:16	Hook in 1.5s, tight pacing

◈ Use tools like **CapCut**, **InShot**, or **Descript** to format and export videos in platform-specific styles. Add logos, watermarks, or emojis for flair and brand recall.

C. Automation Tools

- **Repurpose.io** – Automates cross-posting and resizing across platforms
- **Metricool** – Multi-platform scheduler with performance insights
- **Canva Pro** – Create consistent branding across vertical thumbnails

2. Cross-Promoting YouTube Videos to Maximize Exposure

YouTube remains your **content HQ**—the hub where storytelling, monetization, and long-form engagement happen. Every other platform should **funnel traffic back** to YouTube, where your AI cat truly shines.

A. CTA Strategy

- **Use captions and pinned comments**:
  - "Full story on YouTube ⯑"
  - "Want to meet FluffBot's evil twin? Link in bio."
- **Add a CTA watermark or end screen** linking to your full video.
- Create **cross-platform mini-series** where the final part is only on YouTube.

B. Playlist Teasers

- Break a long-form series into:
  - Part 1: Reels/Shorts
  - Part 2: TikTok exclusive
  - Part 3: Full video on YouTube
- Drive binge behavior and follow-through.

C. Collaborations Across Platforms

- Partner with other creators to do:
    - **Duets on TikTok**
    - **Stitch-style reactions**
    - **Instagram Collab posts**
- Ask them to shout out your YouTube channel in return for cross-platform boosts.

◈ Use trending challenges to introduce your AI cat's personality to new audiences, then redirect traffic to deeper content on YouTube.

3. Engaging With Audiences Through AI-Generated Responses

Comments and messages = algorithmic gold. But responding at scale can be exhausting... unless you use **AI to generate in-character responses** that deepen engagement and fuel the fandom.

A. Using AI for Social Engagement

- **ChatGPT**: Train it on your cat's personality to auto-generate witty or meaningful replies.
- **Typewise AI**: Predictive, tone-aware typing assistant for DMs and comments.
- **ManyChat or Chatfuel**: Create **automated Instagram and Facebook DM bots** for engagement campaigns.

B. Fan Interaction Templates

Situation	AI Cat Reply Example
"I love this cat!"	"Of course you do. I'm 97% adorable, 3% chaos. ⍰"
"What's the next video?"	"Uploading from the glitch vault tomorrow. Buckle up."
"How did you make this?"	"Magic, memes, and more AI than your WiFi can handle."

⍰ *Bonus Tip*: Collect comment data to learn what fans love. Use AI to generate content ideas directly from top-performing interactions.

4. The 30-Day Launch Roadmap – Build Your AI Cat Empire from Scratch

If you're just starting—or rebuilding—your AI cat content brand, here's a **step-by-step plan to go live, grow fast, and scale smart in 30 days or less**:

◈ Week 1: Foundation & Character Development

- Define your cat's niche, backstory, personality, and voice
- Choose your tools: ChatGPT, ElevenLabs, Kaiber, Runway, Descript, etc.
- Create your cat's visual identity (design, logo, avatar, name)
- Record a sample voice and script a short intro video

◈ Week 2: Content Creation Pipeline

- Batch create 3–5 YouTube Shorts
- Create 1 long-form video (3–8 mins) introducing your cat's story
- Repurpose Shorts for TikTok, IG Reels, and Facebook Shorts
- Set up your YouTube channel branding, banner, and playlists

◈ Week 3: Engagement & Automation Setup

- Build your YouTube upload calendar
- Set up auto-posting with Metricool or Repurpose.io
- Create a Discord server or fan hub
- Use ChatGPT to script in-character comment replies
- Launch your first community post or poll

◈ Week 4: Launch & Expand

- Post daily Shorts and cross-platform Reels
- Publish at least 2 long-form videos
- Engage in comments (AI-assisted if needed)
- Promote across social platforms
- Begin building an email list or newsletter
- Launch basic merch or a digital download (wallpaper pack, voice lines)

◈ By Day 30, you should have:

- A growing multi-platform audience
- A content machine running on AI + systems
- Fans starting to interact, create memes, and follow the story
- Your monetization paths in place (YouTube, affiliate, merch, Patreon)
- Your first superfans helping fuel word-of-mouth growth

In Summary

Expanding your AI cat brand across social platforms is not just about visibility—it's about **ecosystem dominance**. By repurposing smartly, cross-promoting strategically, and engaging deeply using AI-powered responses, you multiply your growth while keeping your workload lean and efficient.

Pair this strategy with the 30-day launch roadmap and you've got everything you need to build, grow, and scale a **multi-platform AI content empire**—one that entertains, earns, and evolves 24/7.

Chapter 11: Scaling Beyond YouTube – Merch, AI Cat Apps & More

By now, you've built a content engine, developed a viral-worthy AI cat character, and expanded your brand across multiple platforms. But the journey doesn't end with views and subscribers. The next phase is about **scaling beyond YouTube**—transforming your AI cat from a content asset into a **digital product powerhouse, virtual pet brand, and interactive app experience** that earns around the clock.

In this chapter, we'll explore how to create and sell AI cat-themed digital products, build a scalable virtual pet IP (intellectual property), develop monetized app experiences, and deploy chatbots and AI companions. At the end, we'll **pull everything together into a master blueprint**—a complete vision for sustaining, scaling, and **future-proofing your AI cat brand** for long-term success.

1. Creating & Selling AI Cat-Themed Digital Products

Digital products are low-cost to produce, high-margin, and scalable to infinity. They also allow fans to own a piece of your brand in a meaningful way.

A. Types of Digital Products You Can Offer

Product Type	Examples	Monetization Strategy
Downloadables	Wallpapers, avatar packs, sticker sheets	Sell on **Gumroad**, **Ko-fi**, or Etsy
Voice Packs	AI-generated voice lines, meow soundboards, character greetings	Great for streamers or fans
Printable Merch	Coloring books, comic panels, fan art templates	Add as bonuses on Patreon
Digital Artbooks	AI cat concept art, backstory, worldbuilding	Great as part of NFT bundles
Interactive PDFs	Mystical "Cat Oracle" tarot guides, puzzle books, journals	Sell as fan-lore content or collectibles

⟐ *Tip*: Use tools like **Canva**, **Midjourney**, **ChatGPT**, and **Runway** to generate art and layout your digital products.

B. Selling Platforms & Tools

- **Gumroad**: Best for indie creators selling digital files.
- **Payhip**: Built-in store templates and EU VAT handling.
- **Etsy (Digital)**: Great for downloadable planners, art, and fan bundles.
- **Shopify + SendOwl**: For a branded digital storefront with secure file delivery.

C. Pricing Strategy

- Offer **free downloads** as email capture tools.
- Use **tiered pricing** for deluxe bundles (voice + art + lore).
- Sell **limited-time or seasonal packs** (Halloween cat skins, holiday wallpapers).

2. Building an AI-Powered Virtual Pet Brand

Your AI cat isn't just a character—it can evolve into a **branded virtual pet IP**, similar to Tamagotchi, Neopets, or Pokémon, but designed for the next generation of digital natives.

A. Define Your Brand Identity

- **Species & Variants**: FluffBot, GlitchKitten, OraclePaw—give them types, stats, or moods.
- **Lore**: Build a narrative world—cosmic cats, data realms, emotional AI zones.
- **Merch Tie-ins**: Design plushies, apparel, and accessories to match each version.

B. Licensing & Franchise Expansion

- Develop a **style guide** for partners (logos, character rules, tone of voice).
- Pitch to brands for collaboration (e.g., pet food, gamer gear, AI startups).
- Offer limited-use commercial licenses for fans or indie creators to build their own content around your cat universe.

◈ Consider starting a **"Creator Kit"** with PNGs, brand colors, and voice samples to encourage UGC (user-generated content).

3. Monetizing Through App Development & AI Chatbot Cats

Apps are the holy grail of brand engagement. They live on your audience's devices, allow for recurring monetization, and deliver high-intimacy interaction.

A. App Ideas for Your AI Cat Brand

App Type	Features	Monetization
Virtual Pet App	Feed, groom, play with your AI cat. Unlock new accessories or outfits.	In-app purchases, skins, ad-supported free version
AI Cat Oracle	Ask questions, get fortunes or affirmations from your cat	Tiered pricing for premium readings
Chatbot Companion	Talk to your cat using GPT-powered personality	Monthly subscription
Mini Game Arcade	Tap games, puzzles, music games featuring your cat	One-time purchase or in-app ads
AR Companion	Use your camera to place your AI cat in the real world (Instagram/TikTok filters or ARKit apps)	Freemium, branded collectibles

B. No-Code & Low-Code App Builders

- **Adalo**, **Thunkable**, or **Glide** – Great for MVP (minimum viable product) apps.
- **Unity + ChatGPT API** – For advanced, gamified AI cat worlds.
- **Voiceflow** or **Botpress** – Build voice and text-based chatbot experiences.

◈ *Launch Strategy*: Start with a **web app or chatbot**, then expand into iOS/Android with user feedback.

4. Master Blueprint: Sustaining, Scaling & Future-Proofing Your AI Cat Brand

Here's how everything you've learned comes together to build an unstoppable empire:

◈ Phase 1: Foundation & Content Engine

- Create your AI cat persona (design, voice, lore).
- Use AI tools to automate video production and posting.
- Grow on YouTube, TikTok, IG Reels, and Facebook Shorts.
- Engage fans with AI-generated replies and livestreams.

◈ Phase 2: Monetization & Community

- Activate YouTube monetization, memberships, and Super Chats.
- Launch digital product store (voice packs, wallpapers, lore PDFs).
- Open a fan Discord, start weekly fan features and polls.
- Begin collaborating with brands and creators.

◈ Phase 3: Brand Expansion & App Development

- Turn your AI cat into a virtual pet brand with lore and variants.
- Launch a simple chatbot or virtual pet app.
- Sell seasonal merch, launch NFTs or collectibles.
- Experiment with interactive storytelling, AR filters, or mini-games.

◈ Phase 4: Long-Term Growth & IP Scaling

- License your characters or create a franchise-style playbook.
- Partner with developers for a full game or metaverse integration.
- Continue testing new platforms (Twitch, VR, Amazon AMP).
- Publish a book, digital comic, or web series starring your AI cat universe.

In Summary

Your AI cat isn't just a content creator—it's a brand, a character, a product, and a digital experience waiting to happen. From repurposed Shorts to virtual pet apps, from YouTube monetization to chatbot subscriptions, the growth potential is exponential when you think like a **media entrepreneur** instead of just a creator.

This is your master blueprint:

- **Automate production**
- **Engage emotionally**
- **Diversify income**
- **Expand across platforms**
- **Scale with tech**
- **Own your IP**

You're not just building an AI cat channel—you're creating a **future-proof digital empire** that entertains, engages, and earns across generations of technology and audience trends.

Chapter 12: The Future of AI Content Creation – Staying Ahead of the Curve

The world of AI-generated content is evolving faster than ever—and those who stay ahead of the curve will lead the next wave of creators, brands, and entertainment empires. What started as cute AI cat videos and meme-worthy animations is quickly transforming into **fully immersive experiences, sentient-feeling personalities, and monetizable virtual identities.**

As the tools become smarter and more accessible, the line between **creator and coder**, **influencer and algorithm**, **pet and platform** will blur. Those who understand where the industry is going won't just survive—they'll **scale, pivot, and dominate.**

In this final chapter, we'll dive into upcoming trends in AI-generated video, music, and personalities; explore the rise of AI influencers and digital pets as lifestyle brands; and map out how to **adapt, pivot, and expand your empire** as the AI revolution continues to accelerate.

1. Upcoming Trends in AI-Generated Video and Music

AI video and music are at the forefront of generative media—and 2024–2026 will bring **massive leaps** in realism, interactivity, and accessibility.

A. AI-Generated Video: What's Next

- **Real-Time AI Animation**:
  - Platforms like **Runway**, **Pika Labs**, and **Sora (by OpenAI)** are making it possible to generate entire video scenes from text prompts.
  - Expect drag-and-drop tools for building full cinematic universes—no editing skills needed.
- **Personalized Content at Scale**:
  - Videos dynamically tailored to user data (names, preferences, language).
  - Your AI cat could greet fans by name, deliver personalized jokes, or create custom lore paths.
- **Interactive Storytelling**:
  - Viewers choose outcomes (like a Netflix "Bandersnatch" experience) powered by GPT and animation pipelines.
  - AI cats could evolve differently based on fan interactions or voting.
- **Multimodal Content Generation**:
  - Combine **text, voice, music, and visuals** into a single workflow using unified AI models.
  - Create a full episode in minutes—with consistent tone, pacing, and emotional impact.

B. AI Music: Real Artists Meet Real-Time Remixes

- **AI music will become adaptive and contextual**—changing in real time to match video pacing or user mood.
- **Music licensing will shift** to AI-authored libraries with smart royalties or blockchain-based attribution.
- Your AI cat could **release full albums**, remix user-submitted vocals, or host interactive music experiences.

◈ *Future-Proof Tip*: Start training your own **custom AI sound pack or visual model** now. Owning your style = owning your future.

2. The Future of AI Influencers and Virtual Pets

We are entering the **AI influencer era**—where the most beloved, scalable, and drama-free online personalities are synthetic.

A. Rise of AI Influencers

- AI influencers already have millions of followers (Lil Miquela, CodeMiko, etc.).
- The next generation will:
    - Be multilingual out of the box.
    - Scale to every platform simultaneously.
    - Auto-adapt to trends, news, and culture shifts.

B. Virtual Pets = Emotional AI Companions

- AI cats won't just entertain—they'll **comfort, guide, and bond** with users like digital therapy animals.
- Expect:
    - **Companion apps** with adaptive personalities.
    - **Wearables integration** (smart collars, haptic toys).
    - **AR overlays** to project your cat into your room via glasses or phone.

C. Commercial Applications of Virtual Characters

- AI pet personalities will be **brand mascots**, **sales agents**, **customer service bots**, and **education tools**.
- Your cat could teach language, guide meditation, or host a kids' coding class.

◈ *Future-Proof Tip*: Think of your AI cat as an **IP franchise**, not just a content creator. Merch, books, games, and apps are all future revenue verticals.

3. Pivoting and Scaling as AI Evolves

The tools, platforms, and audience behaviors will change. The only constant? Your brand's ability to **adapt and evolve**.

A. Keep a Fluid Brand Identity

- Build your AI cat to be **multi-version and multi-form**:
  - Baby form for kids' apps
  - Glitch version for meme culture
  - Oracle form for wellness/lifestyle fans
- Evolve the character design or voice as tech allows more realism.

B. Diversify Platforms Early

- Invest in **emerging platforms** like:
  - **VRChat**, **Decentraland**, or **Spatial** for immersive experiences
  - **Twitch** for AI VTube-style livestreams
  - **Web3 & AI marketplaces** for ownership, tokenized lore, and fan-collaboration NFTs

C. Build for User-Created Worlds

- Open your IP to fans:
  - Let them create their own AI cat variants
  - License the brand for games or comic creation
  - Build AI tools so fans can "talk to" or "train" their own cats in your universe

D. Focus on Evergreen Systems

- Automate video production using future-proofed AI tools
- Maintain a **content library that's modular**, remixable, and updatable
- Use tools like **Notion**, **ChatGPT APIs**, and **Zapier** to build backend systems that run your empire

◈ *Future-Proof Tip*: Future creators will be **system builders, not just storytellers**. Your job is to design ecosystems where your AI cat can evolve—across formats, timelines, and technologies.

4. Sustaining the Empire: Long-Term Vision

To sustain your AI cat brand for the long haul, anchor your strategy on three pillars:

1. Community

- Keep building emotional resonance.
- Let fans shape the lore.
- Reward loyalty with deeper access (custom NFTs, app features, meetups).

2. Creativity

- Never stop testing new formats.
- Launch side characters, remix old videos with new tools.
- Evolve the story as the world evolves.

3. Consistency

- Stay visible with content drops (even automated ones).
- Show up on new platforms early.
- Keep your workflows lean and AI-assisted.

In Summary: A New Era of Digital Creators

We're at the dawn of a new digital frontier—**where creators, characters, and algorithms merge**. In this world, your AI cat isn't just a content creator. It's a:

- Brand
- Digital product
- Emotional companion
- Cultural icon
- Monetized, scalable, and evolving media asset

By embracing the future of AI, automating wisely, engaging emotionally, and thinking like a digital architect, you're not just building videos—you're building an **empire that outlives platforms and trends**.

This is your final blueprint. The tools are ready. The roadmap is here. Your audience is waiting.

It's time to unleash your AI cat—and rule the future.

Appendix A: The Ultimate AI Creator's Resource List

Whether you're just starting or scaling your AI-powered brand, having the **right tools** is half the battle. This appendix is your go-to reference for the most effective platforms, software, and AI systems across **video production, music creation, branding, and content marketing**—all optimized for building your AI cat empire.

In addition, you'll find a **30-day launch checklist** to guide you from idea to execution, complete with essential milestones and recommended tools at every step.

1. Best Tools & Platforms for AI Content Creation

⯑ Scriptwriting & AI Voice Generation

Tool	Function	Why It's Great
ChatGPT (GPT-4)	Scriptwriting, character dialogue, content ideas	Best for generating in-character scripts fast
Claude AI	Long-form and emotionally rich writing	Great for lore and storytelling scripts
ElevenLabs	AI voice cloning & ultra-realistic voiceovers	Create custom voices for your AI cat
PlayHT	Voiceover generation with tone control	Multilingual voice capabilities

◈ AI Video & Animation Tools

Tool	Function	Why It's Great
Runway ML	AI video editing, background removal, effects	Drag-and-drop video magic
Kaiber	Text-to-video generation	Stylish, music-synced animations
Pika Labs	AI-powered motion visuals from text	Perfect for short-form storytelling
Genmo.ai	Image-to-animation platform	Animate static cat designs with movement
Adobe Character Animator	Real-time character animation with facial sync	Ideal for VTuber-style talking cats

◈ Design & Branding Tools

Tool	Function	Why It's Great
Canva Pro	Thumbnails, social media branding, templates	Fast, easy, drag-and-drop branding
Midjourney	AI image generation (via Discord)	Create unique AI cat artwork and environments
Leonardo.ai	Concept art generation & image refinement	Ideal for professional-grade brand visuals
Looka	Logo design using AI	Quickly design your cat's logo and brand pack

◈ AI Music & Sound Design Tools

Tool	Function	Why It's Great
Soundraw	AI music generator based on mood and genre	Royalty-free music for videos
Mubert	Infinite loops, royalty-free tracks	Ideal for background music and Shorts
AIVA	Composes cinematic scores	Great for storytelling and dramatic flair
Boomy	Full music production and vocal synthesis	Create original cat-themed songs or intros

◈ Marketing, Scheduling, & Analytics Tools

Tool	Function	Why It's Great
TubeBuddy	YouTube SEO, tags, and analytics	Boosts visibility and search ranking
vidIQ	Trend alerts, keyword optimization	AI-powered insights for viral growth
Metricool	Multi-platform content scheduling	Plan posts across YouTube, IG, TikTok, Facebook
Repurpose.io	Automates content resizing and reposting	Save time cross-promoting videos

◈ Engagement, Chatbots & Automation

Tool	Function	Why It's Great
ManyChat	AI chatbot builder for Instagram & Facebook	Auto-replies, subscriber funnels, fan engagement
Replika API	Build custom AI chat companions	Create interactive AI cat personalities
Voiceflow	AI voice assistant builder	Build Alexa- or Google-compatible cat apps
Zapier	Connect tools & automate workflows	Set up seamless content and analytics pipelines

◈ Digital Product & Merch Platforms

Tool	Function	Why It's Great
Gumroad	Sell digital downloads and bundles	Easy storefront for wallpapers, art, voice packs
Ko-fi	Fan support, tips, and product sales	Combine tipping with product sales and memberships
Printful / Printify	Print-on-demand merch integration	Custom shirts, mugs, and plushies with your cat brand
Spring (formerly Teespring)	Merch store integrated into YouTube	Sell branded items directly under your videos

2. Launch Checklist: Build Your AI Cat Empire in Under 30 Days

Use this checklist to **launch your AI-powered content brand in 4 weeks**, with daily or weekly goals. Whether you're solo or building a team, follow this plan to go live fast and smart.

◈ Week 1: Brand Building & Setup

- Choose your AI cat's **niche, personality, and backstory**
- Design your cat using **Midjourney or Leonardo.ai**
- Create your **logo, color palette, and brand identity** in Canva or Looka
- Generate a **custom voice** with ElevenLabs or PlayHT
- Open your **YouTube channel** (set up banner, description, and profile)
- Set up accounts on **TikTok, Instagram, and Facebook**

◈ Week 2: Content Creation & Automation

- Use ChatGPT to write 5–10 scripts for Shorts and 1 long-form video
- Generate voiceovers and animations using tools like Runway or Kaiber
- Edit your first batch of videos in CapCut or Pictory
- Schedule your uploads using **Metricool or YouTube Studio**
- Repurpose videos for TikTok and Instagram using **Repurpose.io**
- Set up **TubeBuddy/vidIQ** for SEO optimization

◈ Week 3: Monetization & Community Building

- Launch a **digital product** on Gumroad (e.g., wallpapers, voice packs)
- Set up your **Ko-fi or Patreon** page for fan support and memberships
- Create a **Discord server** for fans and community engagement
- Schedule your first **YouTube Premiere or livestream**
- Set up auto-comment responses or DMs with **ChatGPT or ManyChat**
- Begin collecting emails via a free download offer (lead magnet)

◈ Week 4: Expansion & Growth Strategy

- Launch a **mini social media campaign** using branded Reels and Shorts
- Reach out to 3–5 **micro-influencers or collaborators**
- Begin designing a **simple chatbot** or AR experience using Voiceflow or Replika
- Collect and feature **fan art, comments, or testimonials** in your next video
- Set goals for next month: launch merch, create app MVP, build more lore
- Review analytics using TubeBuddy/vidIQ and adjust strategy

3. Pro Tips for Using These Resources

- **Start simple, scale later**: Begin with free or low-tier plans, then upgrade tools as your brand grows.
- **Build systems, not chaos**: Use Notion, Trello, or Airtable to track ideas, scripts, content, and launches.
- **Outsource smartly**: Use Fiverr or Upwork to delegate thumbnails, editing, or admin work.
- **Test everything**: Track what content resonates most, then double down.
- **Stay in character**: Keep your cat's voice, tone, and style consistent across platforms.

In Summary

With the tools in this appendix and the 30-day launch checklist, you have everything you need to **create, automate, scale, and monetize your AI cat content brand**. Whether you're working solo or with a small team, this toolkit helps you stay focused, productive, and creative—without getting lost in the overwhelming world of tech.

You're now equipped with:

� Proven tools

� A clear plan

� Automation strategies

� Monetization paths

� Expansion tactics

Your AI cat empire is ready to launch. The next move is yours.

Appendix B: Troubleshooting & Growth Hacks

Even the most creative AI cat channels can hit roadblocks. Whether it's slow growth, sudden demonetization, or a frustrating copyright strike, every creator faces setbacks. The key to success isn't avoiding these challenges—it's knowing **how to recover quickly, adapt smartly, and optimize relentlessly**.

This appendix is your ultimate guide to:

- Diagnosing and fixing issues when your channel isn't gaining traction
- Recovering from YouTube penalties
- Leveraging **insider growth hacks** to explode your engagement, revenue, and reach—even from a slow start

1. **What to Do If Your Channel Isn't Gaining Traction**

Slow growth in the early stages is normal, but if you're posting consistently and still not seeing momentum after a few weeks or months, it's time for a strategic audit.

◈ Step-by-Step Growth Troubleshooting Checklist

A. Audit Your Content Hook & First 10 Seconds

◈ Ask yourself:

- Does your video grab attention in **the first 1.5–3 seconds**?
- Are you using **movement, music, or a pattern interrupt** to stop the scroll?
- Is your AI cat doing or saying something intriguing immediately?

◈ *Fix*: Rework your first 10 seconds with better visual pacing, snappier dialogue, or an open-ended question.

B. Improve Click-Through Rate (CTR)

Low CTR = YouTube won't push your video, no matter how good it is.

◈ Check your **YouTube Studio Analytics**:

- CTR below 3%? Your thumbnail or title needs work.
- 5%+? You're in a healthy range. Optimize for retention next.

◈ *Fix*:

- Use **bold, expressive thumbnails** with your AI cat's face front and center.
- Write **curiosity-driven titles** (not clickbait):
    - Instead of "My Cat Talks," try "This AI Cat Just Glitched... Hard."

C. Target Better Keywords & Trends

Your videos might not be discoverable.

◈ Use **TubeBuddy** or **vidIQ** to:

- Research low-competition, high-volume keywords
- Track trending sounds, titles, and Shorts formats

◈ *Fix*: Align video topics with rising search terms + social media trends. Example: "AI Cat Reacts to New ChatGPT Update"

D. Increase Posting Frequency & Consistency
YouTube rewards **active channels**.
◈ *Fix*: Post at least:

- 3–5 **YouTube Shorts per week**
- 1–2 **long-form videos per week**
- Community polls and posts to engage dormant subs

E. Funnel in External Traffic
Sometimes YouTube needs a nudge.
◈ *Fix*:

- Share your Shorts on **TikTok, Instagram Reels, and Facebook Shorts**
- Promote with niche subreddit communities (like r/VirtualYoutubers or r/AIArt)

2. How to Recover from a YouTube Demonetization or Copyright Strike

Demonetization or strikes can be frustrating—but they aren't the end. You just need to take quick, proactive steps.

◈ **If You're Demonetized (YouTube Partner Program Suspended):**

Common Reasons:

- Reused content without transformative value
- Misleading metadata or clickbait
- Community guideline violation

◈ *How to Recover*:

1. **Audit your videos**:
   - Add unique voiceover, story, commentary to AI-generated visuals.
   - Remove or edit content that looks like low-effort or auto-spammed.
2. **Reapply in 30 days**:
   - Rebuild your channel with fresh, branded content (show your character development).
   - Create an "About" video explaining your channel's purpose and originality.
3. **Appeal (if eligible)**:
   - Be professional, specific, and show that you've made meaningful changes.

◈ *Pro Tip*: Monetize externally while waiting via Ko-fi, Patreon, Gumroad, and affiliate links.

◈ **If You Receive a Copyright Strike:**
Common Causes:

- Using copyrighted music (even under 10s)
- Reposting someone else's visuals without permission
- Inadvertently using unlicensed content in background

◈ *How to Fix*:

1. **Identify the asset** triggering the claim via YouTube Studio.
2. **Replace or mute** the offending section using YouTube's built-in editor.
3. **Dispute if fair use applies** (e.g., transformative commentary or parody).

Avoid Future Strikes:

- Only use **royalty-free music** (Soundraw, Mubert)
- Generate visuals using **original AI tools**
- Credit properly if using stock content (and verify licenses)

3. Insider Growth Hacks for Boosting Engagement & Revenue Fast

Once your channel is optimized, use these advanced strategies to scale fast and keep fans coming back.

◈ **Growth Hack #1: Build a Video Series, Not One-Offs**

Create serialized content with a **hook + cliffhanger** format:

- "Day 1: I let my AI cat take over my TikTok"
- "Day 2: It started messaging my ex..."
- "Day 3: The chaos continues..."

◈ Why it works: Viewers **binge-watch** and subscribe to see the story unfold.

◈ **Growth Hack #2: Gamify Audience Interaction**

Turn your comment section into a playground.

- "Comment 'MEOW' if you caught the glitch"
- "Guess the next thing my AI cat will say—winner gets a shoutout"

◈ Why it works: Gamification = **more comments**, **higher retention**, and **fan bonding**

◈ **Growth Hack #3: Remix Top-Performing Videos**

Use your **own successful content** as templates.

- Change music, visuals, or POV (e.g., "Cat Reacts to Comments Pt. 2")
- Convert long-form into Shorts, and Shorts into compilations

◈ Why it works: It's fast, familiar, and data-backed to work again

◈ Growth Hack #4: Leverage Fan-Generated Content
Start a hashtag (e.g., #FluffBotChallenge) and encourage fans to:

- Animate their own cat versions
- Remix your voice lines
- Create memes and reels

◈ Why it works: UGC builds **community**, increases reach, and creates **evergreen engagement**

◈ Growth Hack #5: Add Multiple Income Streams Early
Don't rely only on AdSense. Stack:

- Affiliate links (tools you use for AI)
- Ko-fi or Patreon for early access & extras
- Digital product bundles (wallpapers, art, stickers)
- Print-on-demand merch via Spring or Printify

◈ Why it works: Diversified revenue protects you from algorithm dips

Final Pro Tip: Turn Every Video Into a Funnel
Make every piece of content serve one or more of these purposes:

- Attract new fans
- Deepen engagement with your character or story
- Move viewers toward a **paid product or platform**
- Encourage **comments, shares, or subscriptions**

In Summary

Every creator faces setbacks. The key is to respond with data, creativity, and confidence.

When your AI cat channel slows down: ◈ Audit, optimize, and repackage.

◈ Engage your audience in new ways.

◈ Diversify revenue and stay future-focused.

And when things pick up again?

Double down on what works—and scale it with AI and systems, not burnout.

Your brand is only one pivot away from exploding. Use this appendix as your **diagnostic toolkit and creative catalyst**, whether you're just getting started or rebooting after a setback.

Message from the Author:

I hope you enjoyed this book, I love astrology and knew there was not a book such as this out on the shelf. I love metaphysical items as well. Please check out my other books:

-Life of Government Benefits

-My life of Hell

-My life with Hydrocephalus

-Red Sky

-World Domination:Woman's rule

-World Domination:Woman's Rule 2: The War

-Life and Banishment of Apophis: book 1

-The Kidney Friendly Diet

-The Ultimate Hemp Cookbook

-Creating a Dispensary(legally)

-Cleanliness throughout life: the importance of showering from childhood to adulthood.

-Strong Roots: The Risks of Overcoddling children

-Hemp Horoscopes: Cosmic Insights and Earthly Healing

- Celestial Hemp Navigating the Zodiac: Through the Green Cosmos

-Astrological Hemp: Aligning The Stars with Earth's Ancient Herb

-The Astrological Guide to Hemp: Stars, Signs, and Sacred Leaves

-Green Growth: Innovative Marketing Strategies for your Hemp Products and Dispensary

-Cosmic Cannabis

-Astrological Munchies

-Henry The Hemp

-Zodiacal Roots: The Astrological Soul Of Hemp

- **Green Constellations: Intersection of Hemp and Zodiac**

-Hemp in The Houses: An astrological Adventure Through The Cannabis Galaxy

-Galactic Ganja Guide

Heavenly Hemp
Zodiac Leaves
Doctor Who Astrology
Cannastrology
Stellar Satvias and Cosmic Indicas
Celestial Cannabis: A Zodiac Journey
AstroHerbology: The Sky and The Soil: Volume 1
AstroHerbology:Celestial Cannabis:Volume 2
Cosmic Cannabis Cultivation
The Starry Guide to Herbal Harmony: Volume 1
The Starry Guide to Herbal Harmony: Cannabis Universe: Volume 2
Yugioh Astrology: Astrological Guide to Deck, Duels and more
Nightmare Mansion: Echoes of The Abyss
Nightmare Mansion 2: Legacy of Shadows
Nightmare Mansion 3: Shadows of the Forgotten
Nightmare Mansion 4: Echoes of the Damned
The Life and Banishment of Apophis: Book 2
Nightmare Mansion: Halls of Despair
Healing with Herb: Cannabis and Hydrocephalus
Planetary Pot: Aligning with Astrological Herbs: Volume 1
Fast Track to Freedom: 30 Days to Financial Independence Using AI, Assets, and Agile Hustles
Cosmic Hemp Pathways
How to Become Financially Free in 30 Days: 10,000 Paths to Prosperity
Zodiacal Herbage: Astrological Insights: Volume 1
Nightmare Mansion: Whispers in the Walls
The Daleks Invade Atlantis
Henry the hemp and Hydrocephalus

10X The Kidney Friendly Diet
Cannabis Universe: Adult coloring book

Hemp Astrology: The Healing Power of the Stars

Zodiacal Herbage: Astrological Insights: Cannabis Universe: Volume 2

Planetary Pot: Aligning with Astrological Herbs: Cannabis Universes: Volume 2

Doctor Who Meets the Replicators and SG-1: The Ultimate Battle for Survival

Nightmare Mansion: Curse of the Blood Moon

The Celestial Stoner: A Guide to the Zodiac

Cosmic Pleasures: Sex Toy Astrology for Every Sign

Hydrocephalus Astrology: Navigating the Stars and Healing Waters

Lapis and the Mischievous Chocolate Bar

Celestial Positions: Sexual Astrology for Every Sign

Apophis's Shadow Work Journal: **:** A Journey of Self-Discovery and Healing

Kinky Cosmos: Sexual Kink Astrology for Every Sign

Digital Cosmos: The Astrological Digimon Compendium

Stellar Seeds: The Cosmic Guide to Growing with Astrology

Apophis's Daily Gratitude Journal

Cat Astrology: Feline Mysteries of the Cosmos

The Cosmic Kama Sutra: An Astrological Guide to Sexual Positions

Unleash Your Potential: A Guided Journal Powered by AI Insights

Whispers of the Enchanted Grove

Cosmic Pleasures: An Astrological Guide to Sexual Kinks

369, 12 Manifestation Journal

Whisper of the nocturne journal(blank journal for writing or drawing)

The Boogey Book

Locked In Reflection: A Chastity Journey Through Locktober

Generating Wealth Quickly:How to Generate $100,000 in 24 Hours

Star Magic: Harness the Power of the Universe

The Flatulence Chronicles: A Fart Journal for Self-Discovery

The Doctor and The Death Moth

Seize the Day: A Personal Seizure Tracking Journal

The Ultimate Boogeyman Safari: A Journey into the Boogie World and Beyond

Whispers of Samhain: 1,000 Spells of Love, Luck, and Lunar Magic: Samhain Spell Book

Apophis's guides:Witch's Spellbook Crafting Guide for Halloween

Frost & Flame: The Enchanted Yule Grimoire of 1000 Winter Spells

The Ultimate Boogey Goo Guide & Spooky Activities for Halloween Fun

Harmony of the Scales: A Libra's Spellcraft for Balance and Beauty

The Enchanted Advent: 36 Days of Christmas Wonders

Nightmare Mansion: The Labyrinth of Screams

Harvest of Enchantment: 1,000 Spells of Gratitude, Love, and Fortune for Thanksgiving

The Boogey Chronicles: A Journal of Nightly Encounters and Shadowy Secrets

The 12 Days of Financial Freedom: A Step-by-Step Christmas Countdown to Transform Your Finances

Sigil of the Eternal Spiral Blank Journal

A Christmas Feast: Timeless Recipes for Every Meal

Holiday Stress-Free Solutions: A Survival Guide to Thriving During the Festive Season

Yu-Gi-Oh! Holiday Gifting Mastery: The Ultimate Guide for Fans and Newcomers Alike

Holiday Harmony: A Hydrocephalus Survival Guide for the Festive Season

Celestial Craft: The Witch's Almanac for 2025 – A Cosmic Guide to Manifestations, Moons, and Mystical Events

Doctor Who: The Toymaker's Winter Wonderland

Tulsa King Unveiled: A Thrilling Guide to Stallone's Mafia Masterpiece

Pendulum Craft: A Complete Guide to Crafting and Using Personalized Divination Tools

Nightmare Mansion: Santa's Eternal Eve

Starlight Noel: A Cosmic Journey through Christmas Mysteries

The Dark Architect: Unlocking the Blueprint of Existence

Surviving the Embrace: The Ultimate Guide to Encounters with The Hugging Molly

The Enchanted Codex: Secrets of the Craft for Witches, Wiccans, and Pagans

Harvest of Gratitude: A Complete Thanksgiving Guide

Yuletide Essentials: A Complete Guide to an Authentic and Magical Christmas

Celestial Smokes: A Cosmic Guide to Cigars and Astrology

Living in Balance: A Comprehensive Survival Guide to Thriving with Diabetes Insipidus

Cosmic Symbiosis: The Venom Zodiac Chronicles

The Cursed Paw of Ambition

Cosmic Symbiosis: The Astrological Venom Journal

Celestial Wonders Unfold: A Stargazer's Guide to the Cosmos (2024-2029)

The Ultimate Black Friday Prepper's Guide: Mastering Shopping Strategies and Savings

Cosmic Sales: The Astrological Guide to Black Friday Shopping

Legends of the Corn Mother and Other Harvest Myths

Whispers of the Harvest: The Corn Mother's Journal

The Evergreen Spellbook

The Doctor Meets the Boogeyman

The White Witch of Rose Hall's SpellBook

The Gingerbread Golem's Shadow: A Study in Sweet Darkness

The Gingerbread Golem Codex: An Academic Exploration of Sweet Myths

The Gingerbread Golem Grimoire: Sweet Magicks and Spells for the Festive Witch

The Curse of the Gingerbread Golem

10-minute Christmas Crafts for kids

Christmas Crisis Solutions: The Ultimate Last-Minute Survival Guide

Gingerbread Golem Recipes: Holiday Treats with a Magical Twist

The Infinite Key: Unlocking Mystical Secrets of the Ages

Enchanted Yule: A Wiccan and Pagan Guide to a Magical and Memorable Season

Dinosaurs of Power: Unlocking Ancient Magick

Astro-Dinos: The Cosmic Guide to Prehistoric Wisdom

Gallifrey's Yule Logs: A Festive Doctor Who Cookbook

The Dino Grimoire: Secrets of Prehistoric Magick

The Gift They Never Knew They Needed

The Gingerbread Golem's Culinary Alchemy: Enchanting Recipes for a Sweetly Dark Feast

A Time Lord Christmas: Holiday Adventures with the Doctor

Krampusproofing Your Home: Defensive Strategies for Yule

Silent Frights: A Collection of Christmas Creepypastas to Chill Your Bones

Santa Raptor's Jolly Carnage: A Dino-Claus Christmas Tale

Prehistoric Palettes: A Dino Wicca Coloring Journey

The Christmas Wishkeeper Chronicles

The Starlight Sleigh: A Holiday Journey

Elf Secrets: The True Magic of the North Pole

Candy Cane Conjurations

Cooking with Kids: Recipes Under 20 Minutes

Doctor Who: The TARDIS Confiscation

The Anxiety First Aid Kit: Quick Tools to Calm Your Mind

Frosty Whispers: A Winter's Tale

The Infinite Key: Unlocking the Secrets to Prosperity, Resilience, and Purpose

The Grasping Void: Why You'll Regret This Purchase

Astrology for Busy Bees: Star Signs Simplified

The Instant Focus Formula: Cut Through the Noise

The Secret Language of Colors: Unlocking the Emotional Codes

Sacred Fossil Chronicles: Blank Journal

The Christmas Cottage Miracle

Feeding Frenzy: Graboid-Inspired Recipes

Manifest in Minutes: The Quick Law of Attraction Guide

The Symbiote Chronicles: Doctor Who's Venomous Journey

Think Tiny, Grow Big: The Minimalist Mindset

The Energy Key: Unlocking Limitless Motivation

New Year, New Magic: Manifesting Your Best Year Yet

Unstoppable You: Mastering Confidence in Minutes

Infinite Energy: The Secret to Never Feeling Drained

Lightning Focus: Mastering the Art of Productivity in a Distracted World

Saturnalia Manifestation Magick: A Guide to Unlocking Abundance During the Solstice

Graboids and Garland: The Ultimate Tremors-Themed Christmas Guide

12 Nights of Holiday Magic

The Power of Pause: 60-Second Mindfulness Practices

The Quick Reset: How to Reclaim Your Life After Burnout

The Shadow Eater: A Tale of Despair and Survival

The Micro-Mastery Method: Transform Your Skills in Just Minutes a Day

Reclaiming Time: How to Live More by Doing Less

Chronovore: The Eternal Nexus

The Mind Reset: Unlocking Your Inner Peace in a Chaotic World
Confidence Code: Building Unshakable Self-Belief
Baby the Vampire Terrier
Baby the Vampire Terrier's Christmas Adventure
Celestial Streams: The Content Creator's Astrology Manual
The Wealth Whisperer: Unlocking Abundance with Everyday Actions
The Energy Equation: Maximize Your Output Without Burning Out
The Happiness Algorithm: Science-Backed Steps to Joyful Living
Stress-Free Success: Achieving Goals Without Anxiety
Mindful Wealth: The New Blueprint for Financial Freedom
The Festive Flavors of New Year: A Culinary Celebration
The Master's Gambit: Keys of Eternal Power
Shadowed Secrets: Groundhog Day Mysteries
Beneath the Burrow: Lessons from the Groundhog
Spring's Whispers: The Groundhog's Prediction
The Limitless Mindset: Unlock Your Untapped Potential
The Focus Funnel: How to Cut Through Chaos and Get Results
Bold Moves: Building Courage to Live on Your Terms
The Daily Shift: Simple Practices for Lasting Transformation
The Quarter-Life Reset: Thriving in Your 20s and 30s
The Art of Shadowplay: Building Your Own Personal Myth
The Eternal Loop: Finding Purpose in Repetition
Burrowing Wisdom: Life Lessons from the Groundhog
Shadow Work: A Groundhog Day Perspective
Love in Bloom: 5-Minute Romantic Gestures
The Shadowspell Codex: Secrets of Forbidden Magick
The Burnout Cure: Finding Balance in a Busy World
The Groundhog Prophecy: Unlocking Seasonal Secrets
Nog Tales: The Spirited History of Eggnog
Six More Weeks: Embracing Seasonal Transitions
The Lumivian Chronicles: Fragments of the Fifth Dimension

Money on Your Mind: A Beginner's Guide to Wealth
The Focus Fix: Breaking Through Distraction
January's Spirit Keepers: Mystical Protectors of the Cold
Creativity Unchained: Unlocking Your Wildest Ideas in 2025
Manifestation Mastery: 365 Days to Rewrite Your Reality
The Groundhog's Mirror: Reflecting on Change
The Weeping Angels' Christmas Curse
Burrowed in Time: A Groundhog Day Journey
Heartbeats: Poems to Share with Your Valentine
Dino Wicca: The Sacred Grimoire of Prehistoric Magick
Courage of the Pride: Finding Your Inner Roar
The Lion's Leap: Bold Moves for Big Results
Healthy Hustle: Achieving Without Overworking
Practical Manifesting: Turning Dreams into Reality in 2025
Jurassic Pharaohs: Unlocking the Magick of Ancient Egypt and Dino Wicca
The Happiness Equation: Small Changes for Big Joy
The Confidence Compass: Finding Your Inner Strength
Whispers in the Hollow: Tales of the Forgotten Beasts
Echoes from the Hollow: The Return of Forgotten Beasts
The Hollow Ascendant: The Rise of the Forgotten Beasts
The Relationship Reset: Building Better Connections
Mastering the Morning: How to Win the Day Before 8 AM
The Shadow's Dance: Groundhog Day Symbolism
Cupid's Kitchen: Quick Valentine's Day Recipes
Valentine's Day on a Budget: Love Without Breaking the Bank
Astrocraft: Aligning the Stars in the World of Minecraft
Forecasting Life: Groundhog Day Reflections
Bleeding Hearts: Twisted Tales of Valentine's Terror
Herbal Smoke Revolution: The Ultimate Guide to Nature's Cigarette Alternative
Winter's Wrath: The Complete Survival Blueprint for Extreme Freezes.

The Groundhog's Shadow: A Tale of Seasons
Burrowed Insights: Wisdom from the Groundhog
Sensual Strings: The Art of Erotic Bondage
Whispered Flames: Unlocking the Power of Fire Play
Forgotten Shadows: A Guide to Cryptids Lost to Time
Six Weeks of Secrets: Groundhog Day's Hidden Messages
Shadows and Cycles: Groundhog Day Reflections
The Art of Love Letters: Crafting the Perfect Message
Romantic Getaways at Home: Turning Your Space into Paradise
Purrfect Brews: A Cat Lover's Guide to Coffee and Companionship
The Groundhog's Wisdom: Timeless Lessons for Modern Life
The Shadow Oracle: Groundhog Day as a Predictor
Emerging from the Burrow: A Journey of Renewal
The Language of Love: Learning Your Partner's Love Style
Authorpreneur: The Ultimate Blueprint for Writing, Publishing, and Thriving as an Author
Weathering the Seasons: Groundhog Day Perspectives
Valentine's Day Magic: A Guide to Romantic Rituals
The Shadow Chronicles: Stories of Groundhog Day
Love and Laughter: Fun Games for Valentine's Day
AstroRealty: Unlocking the Stars for Property Success
The Groundhog's Path: A Guide to Seasonal Balance
Groundhog Day Diaries: Reflections in the Shadow
The Groundhog's Light: Illuminating the Path Ahead
Valentine's Traditions from Around the World
AI Wealth Revolution: Unlocking the Trillionaire Mindset
Love Rekindled: Reigniting Passion in Relationships
Single and Thriving: Self-Love on Valentine's Day
Emerald Legends: Mystical Tales of Ireland
Green Alchemy: Harnessing Nature's Magic
The Hearts of Horror: A Valentine's Day Nightmare

The Leprechaun's Guide to Wealth and Wisdom

Dancing with the Sidhe: Celebrating the Otherworld

Shamrocks and Shadows: Mysteries of the Green Isle

Emerald Energy: Harnessing Luck and Growth

The Gingerbread Golem's Valentine: A Sweetheart's Guide to Love and Enchantment

The Celtic Knot: Weaving Life and Destiny

Green Fire: Elemental Magic for St. Patrick's Day

Clover Chronicles: Finding Your Inner Luck

Ireland's Mystical Creatures: A Field Guide

Gingerbread Golem's Love Almanac

Prowl and Thrive: The Lion's Guide to Success

Love Alchemy: Transforming Your Life Through Heart Energy

WORLD DOMINATION: Woman's Rule 3:The New Life

The Midnight Rose: A Guide to Lunar Love Spells

The Forbidden Letters: Writing Your Own Love Prophecy

Luck and Lore: St. Patrick's Day for Modern Mystics

The Green Path: A Pagan Celebration of Renewal

The Dark Architect's Guide to Reprogramming Reality

Prankster's Paradise: A Guide to Harmless Hijinks

Manifest Your Reality: The Law of Attraction Simplified

The TARDIS Owner's Manual: Understanding the Doctor's Ship: *A complete guide to the TARDIS, its technology, secrets, and mysteries*

Starlit Romance: Astrology Secrets for Finding True Love

The Time Lord's Atlas: A Complete Guide to the Whoniverse: ***A breakdown of the locations, planets, and dimensions explored in Doctor Who***

Sweetheart Shadows: The Dark Side of Love and Attraction

February Fire: Reigniting Passion in Every Area of Life

The Self-Love Toolkit: 5 Ways to Embrace Who You Are

February Sparks: Ignite Your Dreams in 28 Days

March to Success: A 31-Day Action Blueprint
Ancient Paths: The 13 Sacred Principles of Dino Wicca
Echoes of Tomorrow: Navigating the AI Revolution
The Wellness Blueprint: Balancing Mind, Body, and Soul
Green Horizons: Sustainable Living for a Better Tomorrow
The AI Wealth Code: How to Make Millions with Automation
AI-Powered Creativity: Writing, Art, and Music for Profit
Extinction Rites: Rebirthing Your Soul Through Prehistoric Magick
Sacred Serpents tarot
Celestial Enchantment blank journal
Star Strains
Culinary Journeys: Exploring Global Flavors at Home
The Hollowvale Curse
The Hollowvale Harvest
The Egg of Transformation: Awakening Your Inner Power
Blooming Into Power: A Wiccan Guide to Spring Awakening
The Nightmare Nexus: The Third Doctor's Perilous Haunting
Digital Detox: Reclaiming Your Life in a Connected World
Ostara's Path: Walking the Spiral of Renewal
The Sacred Hare
Financial Freedom: Building Wealth in the Modern Age
Spring's Cauldron: Stirring the Waters of Change
The Hollowvale Pact
Quantum Consciousness: The Science of Reality Shifting
The Hollowvale Hunger
The Sacred Waters Within: A Witch's Guide to Hydrocephalus Magick
The Raven's Nest: Building a Life of Unshakable Stability
AI and the Human Mind: The Future of Intelligence
The Hollowvale Reckoning
Timeless Love: Building and Maintaining Lasting Relationships

The Raven's Roar: Unlocking Unstoppable Confidence
Raven Sight: Awakening Intuition and Inner Wisdom
The Butterfly Effect: Small Changes, Big Transformations
Taming the Boogeyman: How to Conquer Your Inner Fears
The Magick of Green: Awakening Earth's Energy in You
The Entrepreneurial Mindset: Secrets to Business Success
The Hollowvale End
The Shadow Luck Ritual: Reclaiming Power from Your Dark Side
Spring Magick for Beginners: A Simple Guide to Seasonal Energy Work
Doctor Who: The Hollowvale Conundrum
The March of Miracles: Unlocking Synchronicities in Spring
Unveiling the Cosmos: A Guide to Stargazing and Space Exploration
The Ultimate Guide to Surviving an Economic Collapse
The AI Gold Rush: How to Profit from the AI Revolution
Bastet's Shadow: The Hidden Power of Feline Magick
The Bastet Codex: Unlocking the Goddess's Magickal Secrets
Purring Spells: Harnessing Bastet's Healing Frequencies
Bastet's Nine Lives: Rebirth, Transformation, and Immortality Spells
Primal Currents: Hydrocephalus Magick in the Path of Dino Wicca
The Digital Gold Rush: Mastering E-Commerce and Online Sales
Future Shock: Adapting to the Next Decade of Change
The Quantum Mindset: Think Like a Billionaire
Sacred Motherhood: Awakening the Divine Feminine Within
The Mother's Spellbook: Enchantments for Love, Protection, and Prosperity
The Witch's Guide to Parenting: Raising Empowered and Intuitive Children

The Magick of Motherhood: Reclaiming Your Power Through Rituals

The Pagan Path to Self-Love: A Goddess's Guide to Worth and Confidence

Wild Woman Magick: Unleashing Your Primal Power

The Money Magnet Blueprint: Unlocking Unlimited Wealth

Biohacking 101: Unlock Your Body's Full Potential

The Wild Father: A Pagan Guide to Strength and Wisdom

The Sacred Masculine: Unlocking Your Inner Power

The Druid's Compass

The Warrior's Mindset

The Father's Fire

Odin's Path

Ancestral Bonds

The House That Whispers

The Magician's Code

The Wild Hunt

The Green Man's Path

The Altar of Success

The Shadow and the Sword

The High Priestess's Guide to Energy Healing

The Lunar Mother

The Sacred Self-Care Grimoire

The Womb Wisdom Codex

The Wheel of the Mother

The Witch's Guide to Manifestation

The Q2 Reset

The Ultimate Guide to AI-Powered Passive Income

Escape the 9-5

If you want solar for your home go here: https://www.harborsolar.live/apophisenterprises/

Get Some Tarot cards: https://www.makeplayingcards.com/sell/apophis-occult-shop

Get some shirts: https://www.bonfire.com/store/apophis-shirt-emporium/

Instagrams:
@apophis_enterprises,
@apophisbookemporium,
@apophisscardshop
Twitter: @apophisenterpr1
Tiktok:@apophisenterprise
Youtube: @sg1fan23477, @FiresideRetreatKingdom
Hive: @sg1fan23477
CheeLee: @SG1fan23477

Podcast: Apophis Chat Zone: https://open.spotify.com/show/5zXbrCLEV2xzCp8ybrfHsk?si=fb4d4fdbdce44dec

Newsletter: https://apophiss-newsletter-27c897.beehiiv.com/

If you want to support me or see posts of other projects that I have come over to: **buymeacoffee.com/mpetchinskg**

I post there daily several times a day

Get your Dinowicca or Christmas themed digital products, especially Santa Raptor songs and other musics. Here: **https://sg1fan23477.gumroad.com**

Apophis Yuletide Digital has not only digital Christmas items, but it will have all things with Dinowicca as well as other Digital products.

www.ingramcontent.com/pod-product-compliance
Lightning Source LLC
LaVergne TN
LVHW022227200926
848481LV00006B/2151